Reason in the Age of Science

Studies in Contemporary German Social Thought
Thomas McCarthy, general editor

1. Alfred Schmidt, *History and Structure: An Essay on Hegelian Marxist and Structuralist Theories of History*, 1981

2. Hans-Georg Gadamer, *Reason in the Age of Science*, 1982

3. Joachim Ritter, *Hegel and the French Revolution: Essays on the Philosophy of Right*, 1982

4. Theodor W. Adorno, *Prisms*, 1982

Reason in the Age of Science

Hans-Georg Gadamer
Translated by Frederick G. Lawrence

The MIT Press
Cambridge, Massachusetts
London, England

"The Heritage of Hegel" first appeared in German in Hans-Georg Gadamer
and Jürgen Habermas, *Das Erbe Hegels: Zwei Reden aus Anlass des Hegel-Preises,*
© 1979 by Suhrkamp Verlag, Frankfurt.

"Hermeneutics as a Theoretical and Practical Task" first appeared in German
in the journal *Rechtstheorie,* volume 9, number 3, pages 257–274, © 1978 by
Duncker & Humboldt.

All of the other essays in this collection are taken from Hans-Georg
Gadamer's collection of articles entitled *Vernunft im Zeitalter der Wissenschaft,* ©
1976 by Suhrkamp Verlag, Frankfurt.

This book was set in Baskerville by DEKR Corp and printed and bound in
the United States of America.

Library of Congress Cataloging in Publication Data

Gadamer, Hans Georg, 1900-
    Reason in the age of science.

    (Studies in contemporary German social thought; 2)
    Selected essays from the author's Vernunft im Zeitalter der Wissenschaft,
and two others.
    Includes index.
    1. Philosophy—Addresses, essays, lectures. I. Title. II. Series.
B29.G17   100   81-20911
ISBN 0-262-07085-5   AACR2

KH
4-8-83

Contents

Series Foreword

From Hegel and Marx, Dilthey and Weber, to Freud and the Frankfurt School, German social theory enjoyed an undisputed preeminence. After the violent break brought about by National Socialism and World War II, this tradition has recently come to life again, and indeed to such an extent that contemporary German social thought has begun to approach the heights earlier attained. One important element in this renaissance has been the rapid and extensive translation into German of English-language works in the humanities and the social sciences, with the result that social thought in Germany is today markedly influenced by ideas and approaches of Anglo-American origin. Unfortunately, efforts in the other direction, the translation and reception of German works into English, have been sporadic at best. This series is intended to correct that imbalance.

The term *social thought* is here understood very broadly to include not only sociological and political thought as such but also the social-theoretical concerns of history and philosophy, psychology and linguistics, aesthetics and theology. The term *contemporary* is also to be construed broadly: though our attention will be focused primarily on postwar thinkers, we shall also publish works by and on earlier thinkers whose influence on contemporary German social thought is pervasive. The series will begin with translations of works by authors whose names are already widely recognized in English-speaking countries — Adorno, Bloch, Gadamer, Habermas, Marcuse, Ritter — and by authors of similar accomplishment who are not yet so familiar outside of Germany — Blumenberg, Peukert, Schmidt, Theunissen, Tugendhat. Subsequent volumes will also include monographs and collections of essays written in English on German social thought and its concerns.

To understand and appropriate other traditions is to broaden the horizons of one's own. It is our hope that this series, by tapping a neglected store of intellectual riches and making it accessible to the English-speaking public, will expand the frame of reference of our social and political discourse.

Thomas McCarthy

Translator's Introduction

Gadamer in the United States

Fortunately the work and thought of Hans-Georg Gadamer are no longer unknown in the United States. Not only are translations of his major works available here, but since he became professor emeritus at the University of Heidelberg over a decade ago, his own activity in the United States has been carried out with an abundance, a scope, and an energy astonishing for a man in his seventies and now eighties.[1] One might say that he has had the opportunity to be his own evangelist. He has promulgated the "good news" of hermeneutic philosophy by lecturing indefatigably across the face of the North American continent. The philosophical trends on this Continent during the last fifteen or twenty years rather fortuitously have prepared the ground for Gadamer. In the course of that period, the work of the later Wittgenstein and his interpreters, and of thinkers like Austin and Searle, has become a force to be reckoned with among philosophers of the Anglo-Saxon, linguistic-analytic persuasion. Gadamer himself and thinkers like Karl-Otto Apel have often noted the kinship between this analytic style and Gadamer's philosophy of language.[2] Concurrently the interest of philosophers in existentialism began to give way to a pervasive

and serious concern for phenomenology, whether in the per-
ception-oriented vein of the earlier Husserl or in the more
language- and interpretation-centered vein of Merleau-Ponty,
Heidegger, Ricoeur, and Derrida.[3] Then the shift in the United
States toward a sociologically and politically informed philosophy of action, usually along Marxist lines, began just as Gadamer
himself was being caught up in the debate with the Frankfurt
school and Jürgen Habermas. Finally just when Gadamer, perhaps spurred on by the criticisms of Habermas and Apel, was
in the process of reaching a richer, more explicit apprehension
of philosophical hermeneutics as a practical and political philosophy, the teaching of *Truth and Method* started being taken
up and applied by students from all over the United States
working in the humanities. In retrospect it seems clear that
these developments have borne in upon him ever more sharply
the way the political-practical core of hermeneutic theory also
provides a theoretical as well as practical center for the liberal
arts.

Some readers of this book may have traced the evolution of
Gadamer's thought during these years of activity in the United
States as documented in comments and lectures published in
American periodical literature and anthologies. This collection
of essays provides striking evidence of the ripening of Gadamer's mind in these years. What follows by way of introductory
remarks is directed mainly to relative newcomers to Gadamer's
work. I will try to situate his thought in the context of the
history of philosophy generally and to relate it to at least some
currents within contemporary social and political philosophy.

Gadamer in the Context of the History of Philosophy

Gadamer conceives of philosophy as the peculiar sort of activity
that erupted in fourth-century B.C. Athens and radiated out

from the person and work of Socrates. What has come to be known as philosophy originated in this man's practical and political questions about the right way to live. For Socrates philosophy took on the character of a dialectical ascent by which one uses thought, argument, and friendly conversation in order to achieve an ever more vital harmony between *logos* (what and how one thinks and speaks) and *ergon* (what and the way one is and acts).[4]

One cannot have had much thoughtful contact with even the briefest of the dialogues of Plato, who offers us the most paradigmatic contact with the words and deeds of Socrates, without sensing that the philosophic mode of posing the practical and political questions could not be satisfied in the hitherto traditional way — by the myths, stories, and rituals that lie at the heart of any culture. If philosophy always set out from such convictions or opinions (*doxa*), it could not rest there. Indeed the process and term of dialectic was the exacting one of giving an account (*logon tithenai*). But what could count as a philosophically respectable account had to meet newly apprehended exigencies of logic, definition, and inference, which, since Aristotle, we have come to associate with theoretical labor.

Whatever philosophic account claimed to respond to the practical and political questions about the right way to live clearly had to answer the very same questions to which the myths, stories, and rituals had been intended as answers: Why is there anything at all and not nothing? Why are things the way they are? In the writings of Plato, the asking and answering of these questions was never dissociated from the question about the right way to live. But Aristotle differentiated the former questions from the practical and political issue. They pertain to the strictly theoretic sciences (physics, biology, psychology, and metaphysics, though Aristotle never used this last term). By way of oversimplification, perhaps, one might say that henceforth philosophy came under the auspices of "first philosophy," which was dedicated to the question about being as such and so established the basic conceptual framework for all the other branches of theoretic science. Not until the rise of modern science — specifically of a physics whose basic terms and relations were neither dependent upon nor a subset of any explicit metaphysical framework, be it Aristotelian, Platonic, Epicurean, Stoic, Thomist, or Scotist, among others — did the philosophic question about being get displaced from its position of primacy.

After Bacon, Descartes, Hobbes, and Locke, the question about being was no longer primary. Indeed the basic distinctions of metaphysical systems had always tended to be a matter of dispute, and the solutions to these conflicts often seemed to be the formulation of a further refinement or distinction possessing no more than a verbal or notional validity. Hence the animus behind the slogan of the new scientist-philosophers of the seventeenth century: Things, not words. So, too, the first question of philosophy became epistemological: What is the status of our knowledge? How do we know we know? Before a philosopher could squarely face the question about being, he had to dispose methodically of the question about knowing. As a result, philosophy devolved into an epistemology of the positive sciences; instead of being the handmaiden of theology, it became the servant of the so-called modern sciences.

During the late nineteenth century and within the academies of Europe, this state of affairs was epitomized by the then-dominant schools of Neo-Kantianism (mentioned rather often in the essays that follow). Neo-Kantian philosophy was a heady blend of Kantian critique and Hegelian ambition. It formed the primary element within the philosophic climate in German-speaking universities at the time when Gadamer was a young doctoral student at Marburg, working on his dissertation under one of its most illustrious representatives, Paul Natorp.

Part of the great charm, as well as the deep interest of Gadamer's thought for us today, stems, I believe, from the fact that
his career spans the great cultural and philosophical shift from
the nineteenth to the twentieth century. This shift is commonly
dated from the start of World War I in 1914. Thus Gadamer
was bred, educated, and trained as a typical middle-class youth
of the age of Victoria and Wilhelm. His young mind was shaped
indelibly by an intensive study of languages, ancient and modern, and even more so by the mastery of the Greek and Latin
classics. The picture given us by Gadamer of the circle of young
scholars, students, and teachers at Marburg who met each
Thursday evening in the parlor of theologian Rudolf Bultmann
to read through and discuss the entire cycle of the classics of
antiquity is one that is almost unimaginable under the circumstances of the modern university of our day.[5] But Gadamer
does not encounter us as one trying nostalgically to reconstitute
the past in the present. In fact, it is no less typical of Gadamer
that although his dissertation was on Plato, while he was a
teenager he was intrigued by Plato through having been exposed to the anti-Platonic polemics of Nietzsche. In other words
Gadamer's lifelong study of Plato has nothing about it of anti-
quarian enthusiasm or nostalgia. Brought up as he was in the
older world, he was also sharing in a new mood — a mood that,
as he later put it, marked "the end of the age of liberalism with
its belief in progress based on science."[6] As we know now, the
Lebensphilosophie of Dilthey, dialectical theology's critique of liberal theology, the reception in Germany of the works of Kierkegaard and Dostoevsky, the emergence of expressionism in
both life and art — all these things were ushering in a new
epoch.

In philosophy, the arrival of this epochal shift was characterized by the critique of the presuppositions of philosophy under

the reign of epistemology, or of what is now being called foundationalism.[7] First, Martin Heidegger undertook the grand *démontage* of the largely Cartesian assumptions of the then-dominant philosophy. But Heidegger went beyond Husserl not merely in questioning the premise of philosophy altogether but in attempting to uproot the entire tradition of philosophy. The twenty-two-year-old Gadamer, who had just completed his doctoral dissertation, was quick to realize that this involved a contact with what might be called the raw flesh of the original Platonic and Aristotelian impulse without the skin and clothing supplied by the centuries-long accretions of the schools. Whereas Heidegger sought to disinter the roots of philosophy in order to pose again in all radicality the premodern (and even pre-Socratic) question of being, it has been Gadamer's lot to return to the yet more basic practical and political question about the right way to live. This is the main burden of the collection of essays presented in this book.

Gadamer in the Context of Modern Political Philosophy

I suspect that Gadamer has been compelled by the challenge to his rather recently influential hermeneutic philosophy on the part of the critical theorists of the Frankfurt school to a more explicit realization of the practical-political implications of his undertaking and especially of the importance for him of Aristotle's ethics. Still it is certain that this provocation initially did not bring about his discovery of this dimension of his hermeneutic philosophy.

Gadamer's métier as a scholar and teacher had always been the vivid rehearsals in his seminars and lectures of Plato's dialogues. Indeed, from the time of his Heidegger-directed *Habilitationsschrift* on Plato's dialectical ethics,[8] Gadamer's trademark

— in contrast to that of, say, Werner Jaeger and his school —
has been to discern the Aristotle in Plato and to see the Plato in
Aristotle.[9] Thus the centrality of Aristotle's *Ethics* to his thought
was evident not only in *Truth and Method* but also in his earlier
development of that work's problematic in his lecture series at
Louvain.[10] And the inspiration for this motif in his classroom
experiences with Heidegger had been recorded by him in 1964.
Thus he was expressly aware of his affinity for the ethical problematic of Aristotle some years before the now-famous *For-
schungsbericht* in which Habermas made his first trenchant public
comments on *his* magnum opus.[11]

Perhaps the *differentia specifica* between Gadamer's and Habermas's practical-political theorizing may be delineated in
terms of their provenance. Whereas Habermas's conception of
philosophy stands under the sign of Marx's historical materialism, Gadamer's idea of hermeneutics as practical and political
philosophy was inspired by the possibility of a genuine return
to Plato and Aristotle. It is important to bear in mind, however,
how much binds the two thinkers in spite of their very real
differences. Habermas's consistency in attempting to avoid the
positivism not only in Marx's thought but in the social sciences
generally brings his work into harmony with Gadamer's battle
against both the "nominalist prejudgment" entailed by "aesthetic
consciousness" in the first part of *Truth and Method,* and against
the "positivism in the field of history" involved in historical as
opposed to 'hermeneutic" consciousness in the second part of
Truth and Method.[12] In general, the central role played for either
thinker by the reality of communicative practice is emblematic
of the closeness of their different orientations.

Yet there is no denying the stark difference in attitude or
tone between hermeneutic philosophy and critical theory. This
contrast brings to mind a rather touching passage in the fore-
word to the second edition of *Truth and Method,* where Gadamer,

commenting upon the differences distinguishing him from his
mentor, Heidegger, asks:

What does the end of metaphysics as a science mean? When
science expands into a total technocracy and thus brings on the
"cosmic night" of the "forgetfulness of being", the nihilism that
Nietzsche prophesied, then may one look at the last fading light
of the sun that is set in the evening sky, instead of turning
around to look for the first shimmer of its return? [13]

Clearly Heidegger, in his eschatological emptiness/openness,
turned toward and awaited whatever the future may bring; and
Gadamer, in his devotion to the philosophic achievements of
the Greeks, gazed into the past. It does not seem very far-
fetched to locate the utopian, counterfactual anticipations of
Habermas on Heidegger's side of this picture instead of Gadamer's. But this contrast becomes much more subtle when we
compare Gadamer's enterprise with that of his contemporary,
Leo Strauss, the founder of one of the most influential streams
of political theory in the United States today.

Strauss has always taken issue with the claim, often made by
theorists of hermeneutics, of understanding an author either
better or differently from the way in which the author understood himself.[14] Strauss insists that such a claim is meaningless
unless it implies one's having understood the author as the
author understood himself. In accord with this position, Strauss
has proposed the main task of the political philosopher to be
that of understanding the classical works in political theory,
ancient as well as modern, as the authors themselves understood
them. I do not wish to dispute either the logic of Strauss's
argument or the value of his contribution. But the lesson he has
drawn for practical and political philosophy contrasts strongly
with Gadamer's contention that in general understanding what
an author has written always involves understanding differ-

ently;[15] as well as with his strictures regarding the normative character of the intention of the author.[16]

Underlying Gadamer's point is the incontrovertible fact that whenever one understands anything significant (let alone classic texts), one is already engaged in the business of taking up a stance toward the future in the light of the past. Reading, then, is a matter of anticipating meaning and of correcting one's anticipations, precisely because human living already has that kind of structure.

In a letter of 26 February 1961 in which he gave Gadamer his initial reactions to *Truth and Method,* Strauss wrote:

It does not appear from your presentation that the radicalization and universalization of hermeneutics is essentially contemporary . . . with the approach of the world-night or the *Untergang des Abendlands*: the "existential" meaning of that universalization, the catastrophic context to which it belongs, thus does not come out. I am tempted to speak of the hermeneutic situation *par excellence*: the situation which for the first time calls for the understanding of any particular task in the light of universal philosophic hermeneutics.[17]

On 5 April 1961, Gadamer replied:

Where I otherwise still appeal to Heidegger — in this I attempt to think of "understanding" as an "event" — is turned, however, in an entirely different direction. My point of departure is not the complete *forgetfulness of being,* the "night of being" but rather — I say this against Heidegger as well as against Buber — the unreality of such an assertion.[18]

From this exchange it is clear that Strauss interprets Heidegger's apocalyptic strain in terms of Spengler's view of the decline and crisis of the West. Gadamer seems both to agree with Strauss on Heidegger and to link the Heidegger-Spengler position with Buber's thesis of the eclipse of God (*Gottesfinsternis*). For the political philosopher Strauss, then, Heidegger seems to have "opened without intending it . . . the possibility of a genuine return . . . to the philosophy of Plato and Aristotle, a return with open eyes and in full clarity of the infinite difficulty which it entails."[19] In basic agreement with Heidegger, Spengler, and Buber about the contemporary crisis of the West, Strauss set out to retrieve and bring to life the great and classical contrasts between Jerusalem and Athens and between the ancients and the moderns. His aim was to raise the fundamental issues for political and social theory by showing clearly the basic yet radically alternative positions that have emerged. The key evaluative criteria of Strauss's retrieval involve the presence, absence, or relative shape within these alternative views of the notion of nature and the degree to which the various authors espoused what Strauss called "the historical approach."[20] The way authors such as Plato and Aristotle stand on these issues provides Strauss with the "high" in terms of which the "low" of the modern writers may "reveal itself fully as what it is."[21] Hence the overall structure of a *Verfallsgeschichte* that looms so large in Strauss's work.[22]

For Gadamer, Western history is neither simply a story of progress nor one of decline. Although he avails himself of a return to the ancients, he has especially expanded upon another aspect of Heidegger's teaching. For Gadamer, Heidegger's hermeneutics of facticity, his analysis of the finitude of *Dasein,* opened the possibility of a straightforward and explicit acknowledgment of hermeneutic consciousness, the realization that there is no such thing as a privileged standpoint either past or present, no pure counterpositions from which we can learn nothing, and no pure positions in which we need not be critically aware of possible limitations. From the perspective of hermeneutic consciousness, this holds true both for the student as well as for the human realities — even nature — being studied. This is why the whole enterprise of making sense out of the way people have made sense of their lives has a circular and self-correcting character. Understanding authors, texts, and the realities intended by their words is therefore always a function of self-understanding. Similarly criticism of authors, texts, and the realities intended by their words is a function of one's capacity to be critical of oneself. Gadamer's clarity about hermeneutic consciousness lends his openness to the ancients a style that confirms Newman's famous conviction that "here below to live is to change, and to be perfect is to have changed often."[23]

The key issue to be grasped in assessing Gadamer's position in relation to Habermas, Strauss, or anyone else is the way that Gadamer has used basic motifs from Heidegger's thought to generate a theory of interpretation that would cover the manifold aspects of his years of interpretive practice and experience. The radical character of this apparently modest move derives from the extent to which it reverses the characteristically idealist or epistemologically oriented démarche from theories of knowledge and/or reading (and technical interpretation) to theories of human living and being. Hence Gadamer's philosophical hermeneutics breaks decisively with the idealist and Cartesian assumptions of the varieties of Romantic hermeneutics of Schlegel, Schleiermacher, and Dilthey (not to mention later theorists like Rothacker, Litt, and Betti). Under the influence of Heidegger, Gadamer has grounded his theory of human knowing/reading in a phenomenological thematization of the basic activity of life as human. Because human living at its most primordial is always a process of making sense, the standard dichotomies in philosophy between empiricism on the one hand and transcendental a priority on the other are undercut from the outset. It follows, then, that for Gadamer, this integrally interpretive structure of human life precedes and contextualizes the usual oppositions between the hermeneutics of suspicion (in the vein of Neitzsche, Marx, and Freud) and the hermeneutics of recovery (in the direction of what Paul Ricoeur has called a "second naiveté"). The integrally interpretive structure of human living is *the* condition of possibility, not merely of the two kinds of hermeneutics, but of political and social theory generally.

Thus Gadamer's self-defense against the objections of Habermas in their well-known debate often has the following twist: Habermas, in Gadamer's view, accords a primacy to the hermeneutics of suspicion while incorrectly imputing an overly uncritical stance to his own, more radically integral hermeneutics. This argument is rehearsed more than once in the articles that follow. My purpose in mentioning it here is to form a bridge to my comments on why, although the Heideggerian motifs pervade these essays like an undertow, the focal figures in the bulk of the essays collected here are Hegel and Aristotle.

Gadamer and Hegel

The tendency of Gadamer's reception of Hegel is to steer clear of the extremes represented by either the conservative Hegelians of the right, who might be said to overstress the hermeneutics of recovery to the point of legitimating the status quo, or the Marxist Hegelians of the left, who would make absolute the hermeneutics of suspicion.

At the time of the publication of *Truth and Method,* Gadamer was taking pains to underline those aspects of Dilthey's thought that brought him closer to Hegel's full-bodied conception of objective spirit, and so further from Schleiermacher's psychologism and aestheticism. So, for example, the importance he attaches to Dilthey's reading of the antisubjectivist and antipsychologistic theory of meaning in Husserl's early *Logical Investigations.*[24] Almost the identical issue is at stake in Gadamer's sense of the extraordinariness of Hegel's appreciation of dialectic in Plato, namely, Hegel's spelling out of the antisubjectivist and antipsychologistic implications of the openness of the genuine dialectician, for what is moving in and through, yet ever irreducible to, the subjective standpoints of the interlocutors.[25] Cognate issues come up in Gadamer's championing of Hegel's stress upon the mediational character of experience against Schleiermacher's mythical and aesthetically grounded notion of the immediacy of human experience;[26] of Hegel's critique of the extreme subjectivism and formalism of Kant's moral philosophy;[27] of Hegel's sensitivity to the "substance" ever at work in the unfolding of the world-historical "subject" in history;[28] of the suggestiveness of Hegel's notion of the "speculative."[29]

But I do not want to give the impression that in his profound admiration for Hegel Gadamer is prepared to accept Hegel completely or his teaching uncritically. Clearly Gadamer's openness to Hegel's theory of objective spirit does not extend to his theory of absolute spirit. From the vantage of what is, that is, of what is ostensible within finite human consciousness, the utter self-transparency of absolute spirit is a mirage. It represents for Gadamer the apotheosis of the objectivistic and idealist notion of consciousness that began with Descartes and that, with Heidegger, Gadamer has been out to overcome. This is precisely the point where Gadamer is at one with the Nietzsche-Marx-Freud hermeneutics of suspicion: the privatized, idealist notion of consciousness is not only not concretely ostensible, it is also manifestly mistaken to the degree that it isolates explicit self-awareness from its economic, social, cultural, and linguistic conditions of possibility. I think there is no real disagreement between Gadamer and Habermas on this point. What Gadamer goes on to do, however, is to prescind from the Cartesian and idealist elements of the absolute spirit and make the best of Hegel's theory of objective spirit.

A typical instance of Gadamer's way of doing this comes out
in his disagreement with Marx (and Kojéve) about the most
radical meaning of Hegel's famous dialectic of self-consciousness, the dialectic of master and slave.[30] In Gadamer's view, the
culmination of that dialectic is "something truly universal in
which you and I are the same" and that "will be developed as
the self-consciousness of reason."[31] The tendency of Marx and
Kojéve is to suppose that the "presupposition of . . . liberation
from servitude in the external realm of [man's] social existence"
ought to have been Hegel's last word. But as Gadamer goes on
to argue, "the critical approach which seeks and fails to find the
liberation of the wage-slave from the mastery of capital in the
result of Hegel's dialectic is quite superficial."[32] For the ultimate
and crucial outcome envisioned by Hegel, according to Gadamer, is "having reason or exhibiting reasonableness" as "being
able, in disregard of oneself, to accept as valid that in which no
self can consider himself superior to another."[33] Even though
Hegel conceives of this principle of "the unity of the 'real' and
the 'reasonable'"[34] as spirit—what Gadamer tends to formulate
as any "genuine universality such as ethicality and custom, which
in being taken for granted, unite one and all"[35]—Gadamer
insists that this does not mean: "the approbation of things as
they stand,"[36] the assumption on Hegel's part "that work is only
the work of thought and that what is reasonable would be
realized solely through thought."[37] And he then indicts "the
dogmatic conception of consciousness and of idealism which he
[Marx] shared with his contemporaries"[38] as being at the root
of these misunderstandings of Hegel.

Consequently Gadamer attributes to Hegel the view "that self-
consciousness, as free, must work itself into the whole of objective reality, that it must reach the self-evident truth of the solidarity of the ethical spirit and the community of ethical customs,
that it must complete the actualization of reason as a human

and social task."[39] Insofar as Marx or his followers concur with this formulation, he has no objection. What he is adamantly opposed to, however, is what he takes to be Marx's interpretation of this formulation; that "the path of mankind to universal prosperity" is "the path to the freedom of all."[40] But Gadamer by no means disagrees with the necessity of asking "who could be really free in the industrial society of today with its ubiquitous coercion of things and pressure to consume."[41]

Gadamer and Aristotle

Both Gadamer and Habermas want to overcome the Cartesian-idealist bias in either Hegel or Marx by means of a more adequate and empirically verifiable theory of communicative practice. Some readers of this book may be familiar with Habermas's brilliant and provocative attempts to transform the positivist tendencies within Marx's historical materialism. For example, Habermas enlists the aid of Kohlberg's theory of moral development by extrapolating from or transposing that developmental scheme into a heuristic device for tracing the relation of ego and group identity through stages of social and religious evolution.[42] Throughout all his works one cannot help but note the unmistakable centrality for Habermas of a universal moral system emphatically committed to the Enlightenment and Kantian values of the complete internalization and complete universalization of morality.

In contrast, Gadamer has been making his theories of effective historical or hermeneutic consciousness the underpinning for his explication of the practical-political dimension of "the conversation that we are." As so many of the essays collected here abundantly illustrate, however, the paradigmatic figure in the light of which he takes his practical-political bearings is Aristotle. In fact, right now Gadamer probably would favor as the most adequate formulation of what his philosophical hermeneutics is all about the idea that it is a transposition of Aristotle's practical-political philosophy into the contemporary philosophical context.

Gadamer's Aristotelian moorings may be cast into relief by considering the contrasting attitudes of Habermas and himself toward "the whole of objective reality, . . . the solidarity of the ethical spirit, . . . and the community of ethical customs," mentioned previously in regard to Hegel's notion of objective spirit.

Gadamer's reinstatement of the credibility of tradition, his retrieval of the insight into the Enlightenment's "prejudice against prejudice," is intimately bound up with his critique of the positivist exaggerations of method and modern science. Habermas goes along with a good deal of the antipositivist intent of Gadamer's argument, but he wonders if Gadamer's brief in favor of prejudice, tradition, and authority does not also involve a dangerous degree of overkill:[43] Does not Gadamer's demolition of Enlightenment notions of objectification and distantiation within the natural as well as the human, social, and historical sciences tend to eliminate the possibility of critical moral reflection and judgment? Without critical reflection, argues Habermas, there is no hope of emancipation from the oppressive aspects of objective spirit, which render it an environment of systematically distorted communication. According to Habermas, then, Gadamer does not sufficiently see the need for the sort of reflective judgment by which mature persons may discriminate between the objective lie, which masks itself as a "community of ethical customs," and the authentic "solidarity of the ethical spirit." Gadamer's philosophical hermeneutics does not meet the demands of critical reflection not only for distantiation but also for a social theory that elaborates formalized criteria or standards of judgment. Even and especially in the human sciences, then, a properly scientific moment is a condition of the possibility for enlightened, emancipatory critique. Without such a theory, human beings will be left incapable of passing judgment upon a socioeconomic order whose traditions legitimate the exploitation of the many for the profit of the few. Indeed a highly sophisticated social theory is all the more gravely needed today when a complex and differentiated tandem of science and technology must be neither simply dismantled nor simply ignored but subordinated to human values. For Habermas, then, Gadamer's thought in its main lines, both as it stands and in its tendency and implications, cannot adequately ground critical moral judgment today.

Gadamer's response to Habermas demonstrates just how Aristotelian his conception of both critical moral judgment and its grounds is.[44] From Gadamer's standpoint, Habermas's insistence upon distantiation and science as necessary and sufficient conditions for critical moral judgment is itself a failure in philosophic judgment, for it represents a retreat to Cartesian and idealist oversights. One might say that Gadamer finds Habermas lacking in practical wisdom or *phronesis,* the habit of deliberating well. What has always struck Gadamer as so appropriate to the problematic of critical moral reflection in Aristotle's account of this "directing, controlling, and determining principle in . . . matters, personal and social" is the way it goes beyond the logical ideal of rigor, complete explicitness, and coherence.[45] It stands at the opposite pole from the Cartesian assumption Gadamer fears is implicit in Habermas's position: if the objective reasons for the certainty of any belief or prejudgment cannot be clearly and precisely set forth, then that belief or pre-judgment is doubtful or suspect. As a fallibilist, Habermas does not go to the extreme of equating conscious possession of the truth with the adoption of a proposition only when every possible alternative hypothesis has been logically excluded. Yet Gadamer contends that his ideal of *distantiation* appeals to an exaggerated view regarding the susceptibility of political or practical judgments to reconstruction in universal terms. Now Gadamer contends that the positing of any given practical or political judgment still proceeds rationally, without devolving either into the sort of decisionism that Habermas has criticized in Popper and others or into some kind of equally sophistic consensus. What Gadamer means in this context by rational, however, is not characterized by apodicticity; instead it is strictly analogous with the non-rule-governed deliberation and judgment that Aristotle had described under such headings as *phronesis* and *epikeia*.

The key point of contention here is the way each particular and determinate judgment depends in its rationality upon remote criteria residing in the actual detachment and disinterestedness of the knower in his or her cognitional activities, as well as in the habitual context of one's prior acts of understanding, judgment, and belief. Just because neither of these aspects of the remote criteria and context of any given direct or reflective insight is capable of a fully formalized control, this does not ipso facto render the acts of understanding and judgment suspect or doubtful. This is why Gadamer has found the Aristotelian accounts of preferential choice, practical wisdom, and deliberation far nearer the mark than almost any more recent descriptions.

The prejudice, tradition, and authority rehabilitated by Gadamer are all ways of specifying the expressly social and political dimensions of those remote criteria and contexts for critical moral reflection and judgment. It must be conceded that there is a profound parallel between Gadamer's articulation of this dimension of judgment and Edmund Burke's defense of prejudice, prescription, and presumption in the face of the extremism exacerbated by the Jacobin appeal to natural rights. But I do not think it is correct simply to reduce this so-called rehabilitation to a conservative ideology that would lend uncritical support to the personal and structural evils that arise from the arbitrariness and irrationality of individual and group biases. It is significant that whatever influence Burke's thought has had upon him, Gadamer has chosen instead to invoke Aristotle whenever he wishes to justify or call to our minds what is present, operative, and normative for any given judgment, even though it is never capable of being exhaustively thematized or objectified. Thus, for instance, Gadamer's evocation of Aristotle's *phusei dikaion* (right by nature) is an appeal to the normative intelligibility proper to *ta anthropina* (the contingent and ever-changing sphere of human decisions and human affairs).[46] While the content of what is right by nature does not admit of invariant and algorithmic formulation, its very elasticity and mutability still does not, in Aristotle's view, imply that it is reducible to sheer convention or consensus. That had been the sophistic view against which both he and Plato were arguing.

In his retrieval of the Platonic and Aristotelian battle against sophistry, then, Gadamer neither denies nor underestimates how much the real objective spirit today is infected with systematically distorted communication. There can be no doubt of his insistence upon each person's need to be critical of his or her habitual context of judgments and beliefs and of his or her conscious but not yet known prejudices.

For Habermas, however, the basis of critique or the criteria for judgment do not seem to be able to arise from objective spirit as mediated through one's language or deposited in one's character insofar as in advanced capitalist societies and postcapitalist socialist societies these will naturally be systematically distorted. Instead of any optimism about any society as it de facto exists, Habermas seems to be optimistic about the effectiveness of a practical philosophical discourse based upon an explicitly and formally specified ideal speech situation and in anticipation of the realization of the universal communicative community. Such discourse brings factual norms and values before the bar of universalizability, which is the overriding criterion for the attainment of authentic individual and group identity. As such, universalizability tends to prescind from the values, distinctions, promptings, and recognitions of potentiality that are embodied in the language of any society and internalized in the characters of people within that society.[47] The implication is that inasmuch as any given society has a class structure dividing along lines of a "merely dominant minority" and an "internal proletariat," then the values, distinctions, promptings, and recognitions of potentiality of any person or group are suspect from the outset.

The rather divergent implication of Gadamer's adoption of the Aristotelian approach to the concrete intersection of *logos* and *ethos* is not to deny the distortedness of wage slavery and the pressure to "get consumed by consumerism."[48] But it is to affirm that the social dominance of oppressor and oppressed has not necessarily and completely eradicated the mature person (in the sense of the *spoudaios aner* of Aristotle's *Ethics*;[49]) from society and also that no formal criteria can supply for the acquisition of the sort of character that includes a delicate readiness of apprehension and a habitual flexibility of response informed by an orientation to the true and the truly good. I think Gadamer has no illusions either about the extreme difficulties facing the achievement of such a character in today's world or the rarity of its attainment. And so Gadamer esteems the Aristotelian account of the dynamics of critical moral judgment for its vivid sense that there is no formal criterion or rule by which to criticize or circumvent the remote context of habituation and orientation that is part of any single practical judgment. From this perspective, then, unless some "truth of the solidarity of the ethical spirit and [some] community of ethical customs" are already present and operative in that "conversation" in and through which we exercise critical moral judgment, the self-correcting critique of beliefs/ideologies can hardly occur, let alone exercise a pervasive practical influence.

In summary then, we may say that for Gadamer philosophical hermeneutics as a transposition of Aristotle's practical and political philosophy enters into the problematics of the relationship between the sciences and the life-world and of the theory of science as an empirically grounded metatheory. But this metatheory stands to the various universes of discourse and knowledge (common sense, aesthetic, scientific, technical, political, religious) as an "ethics of judgment." Like Aristotle's ethics, it too is grounded upon the concrete exercise of the well-educated or otherwise well-prepared mind (in other words, Aristotle's *spoudaios, phronimos,* or *pepaideumenos* transposed into the contemporary context); a theory of good theoretical and practical judgment; characterized by what Thomas Aquinas, interpreting Aristotle, calls "the certitude of probability . . . , such as may reach the truth in the greater number of cases, although it fail in the minority";[50] and knowledge in terms of affinity and sympathy, of interest for the entire nature of human being. In spite of the fact that it is not systematic in the usual sense, Gadamer thinks of this metatheory as transcendental in the sense of being relevant to every instance of authentic human judgment. Consequently it can play an architectonic role in the contemporary context analogous to that played by politics in Aristotle's scheme.

In order to suggest the social and political implications of Gadamer's undertaking, I shall conclude by citing from one of the most important essays translated for this book:

The claim to universality on the part of hermeneutics consists in integrating all the sciences, of perceiving the opportunities for knowledge on the part of every scientific method wherever they may be applicable to given objects; and of deploying them in all their possibilities. But just as politics as practical is more than the highest technique, this is true for hermeneutics as well. It has to bring everything knowable by the sciences into the context of mutual agreement in which we ourselves exist. To the extent that hermeneutics brings the contribution of the sciences into this context of mutual agreement which links us with the tradition that has come down to us in a unity that is efficacious in our lives, it is not just a repertory of methods . . . , but philosophy. It not only accounts for the procedures applied by science, but also gives an account of the questions that are prior to the application of every science. . . . These are the questions which are determinative for all human knowing and doing, the "greatest" of questions, that are decisive for human beings as human and their choices of the good.

Notes

1. *Truth and Method,* trans. and ed. Garrett Barden and John Cumming (New York: Seabury, 1976); *Hegel's Dialectic: Five Hermeneutical Studies,* trans. P. Christopher Smith (New Haven: Yale University Press, 1976); *Philosophical Hermeneutics,* trans. and ed. David E. Linge (Berkeley: University of California Press, 1976); *Dialogue and Dialectic: Eight Hermeneutical Studies on Plato,* trans. P. Christopher Smith (New Haven: Yale University Press, 1980).

2. See H.-G. Gadamer, "The Phenomenological Movement," in *Philosophical Hermeneutics,* 130–181 at 173–177; "Hermeneutik," in *Contemporary Philosophy,* ed. R. Klibansky (Florence, 1969). See also Karl-Otto Apel, *Transformation der Philosophie* (Frankfurt: Suhrkamp, 1973), vols. 1, 2 passim, for instance, "Wittgenstein und das Problem des hermeneutischen Verstehens," 1:335–337; and the introduction by David Linge to *Philosophical Hermeneutics,* xi–lviii at xxxiii–xl.

3. Don Ihde, "Language and Two Phenomenologies," *Southern Journal of Philosophy* 8 (1970):399–408.

4. H.-G. Gadamer, "*Logos* and *Ergon* in Plato's Lysis," in *Dialogue and Dialectic,* 1–20.

5. H.-G. Gadamer, *Philosophische Lehrjahre* (Tübingen: Mohr, 1977), 37–39.

6. H.-G. Gadamer, "Philosophie und Hermeneutik," in *Philosophische Selbstbetrachtungen,* ed. A. Mercier and M. Svilar (Bern: H. Lang, 1976), 2:33–67.

7. See, for example, Richard Rorty, *Philosophy and the Mirror of Nature* (Princeton: Princeton University Press, 1979).

8. *Platos dialektische Ethik,* 2d ed. (Hamburg: Meiner, 1968).

9. For a more recent illustration of this trait, see *Die Idee des Guten zwischen Plato und Aristotles* (Heidelberg: Carl Winter, 1978).

10. H.-G. Gadamer, *Le problème de la conscience historique* (Louvain: Publications Universitaires de Louvain, 1963); in English, "The Problem of Historical Consciousness," *Graduate Faculty Philosophy Journal* 5 (1975): 8–52. These are lectures Gadamer delivered in 1957 for the Cardinal Mercier Chair at Louvain.

11. See, for example, H.-G. Gadamer, "Martin Heidegger and Marburg Theology (1964)," in *Philosophical Hermeneutics,* 197–212. Habermas's famous critique appeared in his special Beiheft 5, *Zur Logik der Sozialwissenschaften,* of *Philosophische Rundschau* 14 (1967): 149–176.

12. See the first two parts of *Truth and Method,* "The Question of Truth as It Emerges in the Experience of Art" and "The Extension of the Question of Truth to Understanding in the Human Sciences."

13. *Truth and Method,* xxv.

14. See, for example, Leo Strauss, "On Collingwood's Philosophy of History," *Review of Metaphysics* 5 (1952): 559–586; "Philosophy as Rigorous Science and Political Philosophy," *Interpretation* 1 (1971): 1–9; "Political Philosophy and History," *Journal of the History of Ideas* 10 (1949):30–50.

15. *Truth and Method,* 264.

16. See especially ibid., 482–489, for Gadamer's animadversions to Strauss's letter criticizing his positions in "Correspondence Concerning *Wahrheit und Methode*: Leo Strauss and Hans-Georg Gadamer," *Independent Journal of Philosophy* 2 (1978):5–12.

17. "Correspondence Concerning *Wahrheit und Methode*," 5.

18. Ibid., 8.

19. L. Strauss, "An Unspoken Prologue to a Public Lecture at St. John's in Honor of Jacob Klein, 1899–1978," *Interpretation* 7 (1978):1–3.

20. L. Strauss, "Natural Right and the Historical Approach," in *Political Philosophy: Six Essays,* ed. H. Gilden (Indianapolis: Bobbs-Merrill, 1975), 131–156.

21. L. Strauss, "Preface to Spinoza's Critique of Religion" in *Liberalism Ancient and Modern* (New York: Basic Books, 1968), 224–259.

22. See L. Strauss, *Natural Right and History* (Chicago: University of Chicago Press, 1971), and "The Three Waves of Modernity," *Political Philosophy,* 81–98.

23. John Henry Newman, *Essay on the Development of Christian Doctrine* (London: Burnes and Oates, 1845), 29.

24. *Truth and Method,* 58–63, 192–225 (esp. 215–216), 428–429.

25. H.-G. Gadamer, "Hegel and the Dialectic of the Ancient Philosophers," in *Hegel's Dialectic,* 5–34.

26. *Truth and Method,* 146–150, 87–88.

27. H.-G. Gadamer, "The Philosophical Foundations of the Twentieth Century," in *Philosophical Hermeneutics,* 107–129.

28. *Truth and Method,* xxiv; "The Idea of Hegel's Logic" and "Hegel and Heidegger," in *Hegel's Dialectic,* 54–74, 75–116; "Begriffsgeschichte als Philosophie," in *Kleine Schriften* (Tübingen: Mohr, 1972), 3: 237–250.

29. *Truth and Method,* 283, 414–431.

30. H.-G. Gadamer, "Hegel's Dialectic of Self-Consciousness," in *Hegel's Dialectic,* 54–74.

31. Ibid., 72.

32. Ibid., 73.

33. Ibid., 72.

34. Ibid., 73.

35. Ibid., 72.

36. Ibid., 73.

37. Ibid.

38. Ibid.

39. Ibid.

40. Ibid., 74.

41. Ibid.

Translator's Introduction

42. See Jürgen Habermas, "Können komplexe Gesellschaften eine vernünftige Identität ausbilden?" and "Zur Rekonstruktion des Historischen Materialismus," in *Zur Rekonstruktion des Historischen Materialismus* (Frankfurt: Suhrkamp, 1976), 92–126, 144–199; "On Social Identity," *Telos* (Spring 1974):91–103; and *Legitimation Crisis* (Boston: Beacon Press, 1975).

43. See Habermas, *Zur Logik,* and his other contribution to the work *Hermeneutik und Ideologiekritik* (Frankfurt: Suhrkamp, 1971), now also available in English as "The Hermeneutik Claim to Universality," in *Contemporary Hermeneutics: Hermeneutics as Method, Philosophy, and Critique,* ed. Joseph Bleicher (Boston: Routledge, Kegan Paul, 1980), 181–211.

44. H.-G. Gadamer, "Rhetorik, Hermeneutik und Ideologiekritik. Metakritische Erörterungen zu 'Wahrheit und Methode'," *Kleine Schriften.* Mohr: Tübingen, 1967. 1:113–130; "Replik," *Hermeneutik und Ideologiekritik.* Frankfurt: Suhrkamp, 1971. 283–217.

45. John Henry Newman, *An Essay in Aid of a Grammar of Assent* (Notre Dame: University of Notre Dame Press, 1979), 277.

46. *Truth and Method,* 284–286, 471–473.

47. For an evocation of this concrete yet tacit dimension that is so crucial to judgment, see F. R. Leavis, *The Living Principle: "English" as a Discipline of Thought* (New York: Oxford University Press, 1975), esp. "Thought, Language and Objectivity," 19–69.

48. H.-G. Gadamer, "Über die Möglichkeit einer philosophischen Ethik," in *Kleine Schriften* (Tübingen: Mohr, 1967), 1:179–191.

49. Aristotle, *Nicomachean Ethics,* 1131–32.

50. Thomas Aquinas, *Summa Theologiae,* II-II, q. 70, a. 2.

Reason in the Age of Science

On the Philosophic Element in the Sciences and the Scientific Character of Philosophy

It is evident that what we call philosophy is not science in the same way as the so-called positive sciences are. It is not the case that philosophy has a positive datum alongside the standard research areas of the other sciences to be investigated by it alone, for philosophy has to do with the whole. But this whole is not merely, as is true of any other whole, the whole comprised of all its parts. As the whole, it is an idea that transcends every finite possibility of knowledge, and so it is nothing we could know in a scientific way. Yet it still makes good sense to speak about the scientific character of philosophy. By philosophy one often intends a congeries of such subjective and private matters as the unique world view that fancies itself superior to all claims to scientific status. In contrast to such an opinion, philosophy can be justly called scientific because in spite of every difference from the positive sciences, it still possesses a binding proximity to them that separates it from the realm of the world view based upon strictly subjective evidence.

This is not simply the case from the standpoint of its origin, for at that point philosophy and science are indistinguishably one, and each or both are a creation of the Greeks. With the comprehensive term *philosophy,* the Greeks denoted every kind of theoretic knowledge. In the meantime we use Greek words to talk about the philosophy of eastern Asia or India, but by doing so we actually relate such thought constructions to our Western philosophic and scientific traditions and even try to make sense of completely divergent materials as did, say, Christian Wolff when he articulated the *sapientia sinica* as "practical philosophy."

In our linguistic usage, however, philosophy also means everything that can here be called "the philosophic element in the sciences," that is, the dimension of foundational concepts that determine the objective field of any given science, as for example, inorganic and organic nature, the plant world, the animal world, or the human world. And in its own style of thinking and knowing, such philosophy does not at all intend to lag behind the binding character of the sciences. Although today it gladly calls itself "theory of science" (*Wissenschaftstheorie*), it still stands by the claim of philosophy to be a giving of accounts (*Rechenschaftsgabe*). So the question arises as to how it can possess the binding character of science without itself being science, and especially how it can adequately fulfill the philosophic demand of giving an account today when the logic of research has become sufficiently conscious of itself to forbid any merely imaginative speculation about the whole that is not subject to its rule.

Now one can of course suggest that the mere proliferation of the sciences in every direction, which carries out their idea of method, leaves unsatisfied an ultimate need of reason: to be able to preserve a unity within the totality of what is. Hence the demand for a systematic and comprehensive articulation of our knowledge would remain the legitimate field of philosophy. But just this confidence in philosophy to bring about a labor of systematic ordering meets with ever greater mistrust. Today humanity seems ready in a new way to assume its own limitedness and, despite the insurmountable particularity of the knowledge that science comes to know, to find satisfaction in the increasing mastery of nature that it owes to that particularity.

It even takes into account the fact that with the increasing mastery of nature, the domination of human beings over human beings is not eliminated but, counter to all expectation, becomes ever greater and threatens freedom from within. A result of technology is that it leads to such a manipulation of human society, of the formation of public opinion, of the life conduct of everyone, of the disposition of each individual's time between job and family, and it takes our breath away. Metaphysics and religion seem to have provided a better support for the task of order in human society than the power packed into the modern sciences. But the answers that they claimed to give are for people of today answers to questions one really cannot ask and, as they suppose, do not really need to ask.

Thus something seems to have become true that Hegel, from a position of full engagement with the reality of philosophy, still perceived as an impossible contradiction when he said that a people without a metaphysics would be like a temple without a sanctuary, an empty temple, a temple in which nothing dwells any longer and hence is itself nothing any more. That is it: "a people without a metaphysics!" One can hardly fail to notice that in this phrase of Hegel the word *people* (*Volk*) refers not to a political unity but to a community of language. But then Hegel's statement, which might have excited emotion or nostalgia or even called forth the ridicule of the radical enlightenment types, is suddenly thrust once again into our own time and world situation, and then it has us ask in all seriousness, Does there ultimately reside in the solidarity that unites all the speakers of a language something about whose content and structure one can inquire and concerning which no science is capable of even asking a question? Is it ultimately significant that science not only does not think — in the emphatic sense of the word intended by Heidegger in his oft-misunderstood statements — but also does not really speak a language in the proper sense?

No doubt the problem of language has attained a central position within the philosophy of our century. It has a position that is congruent neither with the older tradition of Humboldt's language philosophy nor with the comprehensive claims of the general science of language or linguistics. To some extent we owe this to the reacknowledgment of the practical life world that has taken place on the one hand within phenomenological research and on the other within the Anglo-Saxon pragmatic tradition of thought. With the thematization of language as it belongs indissolubly to the human life world, a new basis for the old metaphysical question about the whole seems to be available. In this context language is not a mere instrument or a special capacity with which humanity is endowed; rather it is the medium in which we live from the outset as social natures and which holds open the totality within which we live our lives. Orientation toward the whole: some such reality resides in language but not as long as one is dealing with the monological modes of speech of scientific sign systems, which are exhaustively determined by the research area being designated in any given case. But language as orientation to the whole comes into play wherever real conversation occurs and that means wherever the reciprocity of two speakers who have entered into conversation circles about the subject matter. For everywhere that communication happens, language not only is used but is shaped as well. This is why philosophy can be guided by language when it conducts its relentless questioning beyond every scientifically objectifiable realm of objects. It has done this ever since the educative talks of Socrates and that characteristically dialectical orientation toward the *logoi*, which Plato and Aristotle in like manner take as a standard for the intellectual analysis. It is that well-known second-best journey to which Socrates breaks through in Plato's *Phaedo* after the unmediated investigation of things as afforded him by the science of his time left him without any orientation whatsoever. It is the turn to the idea in which philosophy as the conversation of the soul with itself (as thinking in a process of endless self-understanding) is actuated. Even the language of the Hegelian dialectic, which strives to sublate the language rigidly conceptualized in statement and counterstatement, dictum and contradiction, and to raise it beyond itself, succeeds in promoting language through thinking and in being itself converted into language, inasmuch as that is the means by which and in which the concept is brought to conceptualization.

The foundation upon which philosophy in Greece established itself in this way was, of course, the unrestricted nature of the desire to know, but not indeed that which we call science. If the first name for metaphysics was "first science" (*prima philosophia*), not only did such knowledge of God, world, and human being that comprised the content of traditional metaphysics possess in an undisputed fashion an absolute primacy with respect to all the other knowledge (which had its exemplary instantiation in the mathematical sciences, number theory, trigonometry, and music [astronomy]). On the contrary, what we call science for the most part would not have even entered into the scope of the Greek use of the word *philosophia*. The expression *empirical science* would have struck the Greek ear like a sounding brass. One called that history, information. What corresponds to our usual notion of science they would have understood at best as the knowledge on the basis of which an act of making or producing is possible; they called it *poietike episteme* or *techne*. For this the standard example and at once the leading variety of such *techne* was medicine, which we too do not call science so much as the art of healing when we wish to honor the humane aspect of its task.

The theme with which we are concerned here, therefore, embraces in its way the entire course of Western history — the beginnings of science and the critical situation of our day in which one finds a world transformed on the basis of science into a single huge business. To be sure, our question thereby extends at the same time beyond the present world of our own history insofar as we are starting to take it as a challenge that there are also traditions of wisdom and knowledge of other cultural contexts that do not express themselves in the language of science and on the basis of science. Thus it becomes methodically suitable to make a theme of the relationship between philosophy and science in its full scope. This means considering that relationship just as much from its Greek inception as in regard to the recent consequences that have come to light within modernity. For modernity is defined — notwithstanding all disputed datings and derivations — quite univocally by the emergence of a new notion of science and method. This notion was worked out initially in a partial field of study by Galileo and philosophically grounded for the first time by Descartes. Since the seventeenth century, therefore, what we today call philosophy is found to be in a changed situation. It has come to need legitimation in the face of science in a way that had never been true before; and for all of two centuries right down to the death of Hegel and Schelling, it was actually constructed in such a self-defense against the sciences. The systematic edifices of the last two centuries are a dense succession of such efforts to reconcile the heritage of metaphysics with the spirit of modern science. Thereafter, with the entry into the positive age, as it has been called since Comte, one seeks to save oneself upon solid land from the storms of mutually conflicting world views with a merely academic seriousness about the scientific character of philosophy. And so philosophy entered into the bog of historicism, or got stranded in the shallows of epistemology, or goes back and forth in the backwater of logic.

A first approach toward determining the relationship of philosophy and science lies in a return to the time when the scientific character of philosophy was still a fully serious issue. Most recently that was in the days of Hegel and Schelling. In a renewed heightening of awareness concerning the unity of all our knowing, Hegel's and Schelling's systematic projects of a century and a half ago wanted to provide a new justification for science and, vice-versa, to ground Idealism upon science. Schelling tried to accomplish this by his physical proof for Idealism; Hegel by combining the philosophy of nature and philosophy of mind together in the unity of the *Realphilosophie* in contrast to the *Idealphilosophie* of the *Logic*.

It is not as if one could renew this attempt at a speculative physics, which in the nineteenth century was used and abused as an alibi against philosophy. Of course, reason's need for unity and for the unity of knowing stays alive today, but now it knows itself to be in conflict with the self-awareness of science. The more honestly and rigorously science understands itself, the more mistrustful it has become toward all promises of unity and claims of final validity. To gain insight into why the attempt at a speculative physics and at an integration of the sciences into the system of science taught by philosophy has shattered is therefore to come to learn more sharply the range and limits of science.

Hegel and Schelling themselves were not blind to the legitimate claim to autonomy of the empirical sciences, which pursue their own methodical course and which by their own step-by-step procedure have set the new task of the philosophy of the modern age. At the high point of his effectiveness in Berlin, Hegel, in the preface to the second edition of his *Encyclopedia*, told us how he viewed the relationship of philosophy and the empirical sciences and what the philosophical problems involved were. It is simple enough to understand that the contingency of what confronts us here and now cannot be completely derived from the necessity of the concept. Even the extremely rare case of a sure prediction (as is afforded by the large spatial relationships of our solar system for the calculation of the length of day and night, of eclipses, and so forth) contains not only an ever-present margin of deviations (which, of course, any unsophisticated possibility of observation does not miss by more than decimal points). It is more to the point that the appearance of the predicted celestial events in the heaven as such is not predictable, for any natural observation depends upon weather conditions — and who would want to base his dependability upon the weather forecasts?

With regard to such a drastic example, it is certainly not a matter of the universal relationship between a particular, contingent instance and necessity but of an intrascientific problematic. Hegel has shown that a descriptive unity exists between the necessity of the general law and the contingency of a single case. When measured against the necessity of the concept, the necessity of the natural law itself is to be regarded as a contingent one. It is not an intelligible necessity — the way one can perhaps call it an intelligible necessity that a living organism maintains itself in a process of material exchange. In the realm of the investigation of nature, the formulation of mathematically exact regularities is an approximative ideal. It is a rather vague normative image of unity, simplicity, rationality, yes, of elegance, that such propositionally stated laws follow. Their true standard is solely the data of the experience itself.

It would appear that the domain of human affairs is one that chiefly falls into the realm of chance. Historical skepticism is far better supported by experience than by faith in historical necessity and in reason in history. Here the need of reason would remain utterly unsatisfied if one were to appeal merely to the regularities in the course of history, which, just like the laws of nature, are by their own proper meaning (*Seinssinne*) intended only to formulate what actually occurs.

The need of reason means something else, and Hegel's philosophy of world history is a good illustration of this. The aprioristic thought that resides in the essence of humankind and that he comes to know in history is the thought of freedom. Hegel's famous scheme of Orient, Antiquity, and Christian world went something like this. In the Oriental world only one is free, in Antiquity a few, in the Christian world all human beings are free. That is the rational intent of world history. This does not mean to say that world history is intelligible in all the factual details of its historical unfolding. The full scope of phenomena that one can call accidental remains infinite. However the accident is no counter-instance but precisely a confirmation of the meaning of necessity as proper to the concept. Nor is it an objection against the rational intent of world history that the freedom of everyone proposed by Hegel as the principle of the Christian world has not actually come about and that times of unfreedom keep on arising; indeed that perhaps systems of social unfreedom could, as in our own acute world situation, in the end be established in an inescapable fashion. This all falls within the realm of the contingency of human affairs, which nonetheless does not hold good against the principle, for there is no higher principle of reason than that of freedom. Thus the opinion of Hegel and thus our own opinion as well. No higher principle is thinkable than that of the freedom of all, and we understand actual history from the perspective of this principle: as the ever-to-be-renewed and the never-ending struggle for this freedom.

It would be a misunderstanding one encounters often enough to suppose that this rational aspect proper to the concept could be refuted by the facts. The notorious statement, "So much the worse for the facts," contains a profound truth. The statement is not directed against the empirical sciences, but on the contrary, against what Hegel, in the Berlin preface, called the whitewashing over of the contradictions that open up the abyss between philosophy and the sciences. He wants nothing of such a "moderate enlightenment," in which the promotion of science and the argumentation with concepts of reason find themselves side by side in a sort of compromise. That was "only apparently a favorable condition." The peace was "superficial enough." "But in philosophy the spirit has celebrated its reconciliation with itself." Clearly Hegel wishes to say the rational need for unity is legitimate under all circumstances and that it can be satisfied only by philosophy. Whereas science, in pretending to posit itself absolutely, only then enters into an irresolvable contradiction with philosophy. This is exactly the case in our example of the freedom of all. Anyone who does not see that this is precisely what history is, that the freedom of all has become an irrefutable principle and yet still requires ever anew the effort toward achieving its realization, has not understood the dialectical relationship of necessity and contingency and so also the claim of philosophy to know concrete rationality.

We look upon Hegel now not only in the domains of historical science, where his productive contributions have been considerable, but in the realm of the natural sciences, with a much more balanced view. He stood at the apex of the science of his day. The price paid by this and Schelling's natural philosophy to ludicrousness was not its informational status but the denial of the essential diversity of the perspective of reason on things as opposed to empirically grounded knowledge. This lay to be sure on the side of Schelling and Hegel too but far more on the side of the empirical sciences insofar as they were blind to their own presuppositions. An empirical knowledge that knows itself in its conditionedness must in truth take a stand to the effect that within its own field of investigation it stands on its own and is removed from every dogmatic use. It remains a teaching that has never been taken sufficiently to heart until perhaps today: that philosophy cannot be read into the work of scientific research but rather comes to light precisely when the sciences restrain themselves from philosophical supplementations and speculative dogmatizing; and so they keep philosophy too from short-cut interventions into the sciences. Hegel and Schelling are more the victims of dogmatism within the sciences than of their own dogmatic fantasies of comprehensiveness.

When later on Neo-Kantianism as well as phenomenology once again claimed to take as their object the fundamental concepts of extant fields of research with respect to their a priori givenness, the dogmatic claim connected with such an enterprise was, of course, disavowed by the research fields themselves. Chemistry has been taken up by physics; biology has been taken up by chemistry; and the entire classification of the plant and animal worlds has given way to an interest in the transitions and in the continuity of these transitions. Moreover, logic itself increasingly has been taken under the wings of modern mathematics. My own teacher, Natorp, even tried to demonstrate a priori and conceptually the three-dimensionality of space, just as Hegel had done with the sevenfold count of the planets. All that is over and done, but the task remains, for the understanding of our life world as deposited in our language cannot be fully resolved by means of the possibilities of knowledge available to science. Science may be able to bring us to the point of producing life in a test tube or of artificially lengthening the human life span to whatever length. But this does not affect the tough discontinuities between what is material and what is living or indeed between a really lived life and a withering away into death. The articulation of the world in which we live through language and communicative cooperation is neither a completely conventional dimension nor the residue of a perhaps false consciousness; it is constitutive of what is and is for the most part sure of its legitimacy precisely because it has to be assumed by every protest, contradiction, and critique. Over against this context, the dismantling and reconstructing of everything that is which is carried on by modern science represents simply a particular domain of expansion and mastery, which is limited just to the degree that the resistance of what exists to objectification cannot be overcome.

Consequently it cannot be denied that science always has and always will come up against a claim of comprehension (*Begreifens*) in the face of which it must fail — and indeed which it should forgo. Ever since Socrates in the *Phaedo* initiated the flight into the *logoi,* this claim has been fastened upon by philosophy as its own proper task. Hegel stands within this heritage. He too followed the guidance of language. "The language of everyday consciousness" is already penetrated by categories, which it is the task of philosophy to bring to the conceptual level. This is the way Hegel saw the matter. Today we stand before the question as to whether perhaps we can no longer see things in this way because science has liberated itself from language inasmuch as it has developed its own sign systems and symbolic constructs that are not susceptible of translation into the language of everyday consciousness. Are we not heading toward a future in which languageless, wordless adaptation makes the affirmation of reason negligible? And just as science today posits itself as autonomous in a new way to the extent that its influence upon our lives has not been mediated through the common usage of commonsense language, a similar concern arises in a second dimension. As is well known, Hegel took special interest in studying the system of needs as the foundation for society and state, and yet he decisively subordinated this system to the spiritual forms of ethical life. In contrast, in our day we see this system bound up with the vicious circle of production and consumption, which drives humanity ever more deeply into alienation from itself because natural needs are no longer "taken care of" themselves; that is, they may be shown to be more the product of some alien interest than of the direct interest in the satisfaction of a need.

Now one could, of course, ask whether the dedogmatization of science that has occurred in the twentieth century, inasmuch as it began to require a split from natural perception, has ultimately accomplished little more — and that would be useful — than to bar a too facile access to the fields of investigation by the human capacity for imagination. And on the other and more positive side, it has broken the dogmatic seductiveness that arose from this easy accessibility and that Hegel called the whitewashing over of contradictions. The mechanical model that in Hegel's and Schelling's time rested on the sure foundation of Newtonian physics possessed an old-fashioned proximity to making, to mechanical manufacture. And so it had made possible the manipulation of nature for artificially worked out ends. In this universal technical perspective there lay a certain correspondence to the philosophic primacy that had been won by self-consciousness in the more recent development. We are always in danger of uncritically accepting the construction of history elaborated by German Idealism. One must ask oneself whether both views might not fall short. The central position of self-consciousness was basically established for the first time by German Idealism and its claim to construct truth in its entirety from self-consciousness precisely by laying down as the foremost premise Descartes' characterization of the thinking substance with its primacy in regard to certitude. But exactly at this point the nineteenth century has shaken the foundations. The critique of the illusions of self-consciousness, which was inspired by the anticipations on the part of Schopenhauer and Nietzsche and which in the meantime has forced its way into science and lent psychoanalysis its support, is not an isolated fact. And Hegel's own attempt to get beyond the idealistic notion of self-consciousness and to let the world of the objective spirit issue as a higher dimension of the truth from the dialectic of self-consciousness signaled an advance in the same direction in which Marx and the Marxist doctrine of ideology have been headed.

Perhaps even more significantly, the notion of objectivity so closely coupled in physics with that of measurability has undergone profound changes within more recently theoretical physics. The role that statistics has begun to play even in these domains and increasingly affects our entire economic and social life lets new models of self-consciousness come to the fore in contrast to mechanics and power-driven machines. Characteristic of such models is a type of self-regulation that is conceivable less along the lines of the manipulable than of something living, of life organized in regulated cycles.

It would still be a mistake to disregard the desire for mastery expressed in these new methods for dominating nature and society. The immediacy with which human intrusions are felt wherever mechanisms have become completely obvious has been softened by the more mediated forms of guidance, balance, and organization. All of this is apparent to me. But this is something to think about. Presumably one has to regard the progress of industrial civilization that we owe to science precisely under the apprehension that the very power that men exercise over nature and other men has lost much of its obviousness and that this has brought about a mounting temptation for misuse. Think about mass murder or about the war machine that by a mere push of a button may be unleashed to do its annihilating work. But think, too, about the mounting automatism of all forms of social life; about the role of planning, say, for which it is essential to make long-range decisions, and that means removing from our disposal a great deal of our freedom to decide; or about the growing power of administration that delivers into the hand of bureaucrats a power not really intended by anyone but no less inevitable for all that. In this way ever more areas of our life fall under the compulsory structures of automatic processes, and ever less does humanity know itself and its spirit within these objectifications of the spirit.

Nevertheless precisely this situation of the self-crucifying subjectivism of modernity seems to me to lend significance to another dimension, which has been removed from modern self-consciousness with its self-aggrandizement to the point of making life anonymous; indeed which promises a new impact in the opposite direction from old motifs. And in this respect, it appears to me that Hegel manifests a new relevance. He not only brings to perfection the thought of self-consciousness that underpins modernity and stretches this structure of subjectivity over the formations of the objective spirit and of the absolute spirit, but he restores to renewed validity a sense of rationality that stems from the most ancient Greek origins. The notion of reason and of rationality is not merely a determination of our self-consciousness. That notion played a decisive role in Greek philosophy without the benefit of an explicit concept of the subject or of subjectivity, and it remains a constant provocation of our capacity to comprehend Hegel that he set down as the final paragraphs of his system of the philosophic science, without any commentary, a Greek text from Aristotle's *Metaphysics*. Certainly it is a text on which we can hardly help but bring our notion of self-consciousness to bear. The highest degree of self-consciousness must be ascribed to the highest divine being. And indeed for Greek thought the total structure of being peaks in the self-consciousness of the God that thinks itself; and indeed in such a way that within this structure human self-consciousness plays no more than a modest role.

τιμιώτατα τὰ ἀστρα. "The highest in dignity are the stars."

That remains the unshakable standard in the light of which Greek thought sees the position of man in the cosmos. It sounds strange to us that not humanity but the stars should represent the most honored element among all beings. Its tenor is no less distant from Hegel than from our own present. Nevertheless a dialectical relevance lies concealed in this which is worth uncovering and which lends to both Hegel and our Greek forefathers a new significance. Hegel's characterization of philosophy as the reconciliation of corruption then appears less a valid truth or an idealistic untruth than a kind of romantic anticipation. According to Hegel, from the division between self-consciousness and the reality of the world there should emerge the higher form of truth through reconciliation and the unification of oppositions insofar as the subjective element would be freed from the fixity of its opposition to the objective element. That was the eschatological pathos of his philosophy. What surrounds us is, of course, the reverse: the bad infinity of an endlessly progressive, almost as if driven process of determining, overpowering, appropriating. Hegel connected such a bad infinity with the external understandable aspect of the rational world and the stubbornness with which it insists upon the setting up of oppositions. And so it posits what is outward in its opposition to itself, in its sheer objectivity. When, however, Hegel in contrast teaches the true infinity of self-determining being in itself — for example, of the living thing, or of self-consciousness, or of the human race's gradually being liberated to a condition of consciousness of its freedom, or of spirit's becoming transparent to itself in art, religion, and philosophy — one sees oneself transported all at once beyond the crevices of time to an altogether new footing.

If the Greek rationality (which Hegel tried to unite with modern self-consciousness in a new unity) may no longer be seen as a mere foreshadowing of modern rationality, then it is to be construed completely differently. It is no longer the enigmatic self-forgetfulness that has been lost in contemplation of the world and that was only related to itself in the case of the highest cosmic God. In contrast with the bad infinity that exercises such relentless pressure upon us, Greek reason appears as the image of a unique future possible for us and of a possibility for life and for survival. Neither the construction of systems that join together in thought things that have emerged in contradiction with one another nor the measureless passion of the architects of the systematic constructs appears to us to hold up the ideal of reason before our eyes. Puzzlingly enough, the rational need for unity has been repeatedly disappointed by the progress of research and to its astonishment it has learned to find its balance in the midst of a manifold of particularities that each in themselves possess the particular unified structure peculiar to systems. I think it is symptomatic that systems theory has displaced systematic constructs.

What a transformation of meaning of the world *theory* is manifest here! What lies at the root of this change? The word *theory, theoria,* is Greek. It exhibits the distinctive characteristic of the human being — this fragile and subordinate phenomenon in the universe — that in spite of his slight and finite measure he is capable of pure contemplation of the universe. But from the Greek standpoint, it would be impossible to construct theories. That sounds as if we made them. The word does not mean, as it does from the vantage of a theoretic construct based upon self-consciousness, the distance from beings that allows what is to be known in an unbiased fashion and thereby subjects it to anonymous domination. Instead the distance proper to *theoria* is that of proximity and affinity. The primitive meaning of *theoria* is participation in the delegation sent to a festival for the sake of honoring the gods. The viewing of the divine proceedings is no participationless establishing of some neutral state of affairs or observation of some splendid demonstration or show. Rather it is a genuine sharing in an event, a real being present. Correspondingly the rationality of being, this grand hypothesis of Greek philosophy, is not first and foremost a property of human self-consciousness but of being itself, which is the whole in such a way and appears as the whole in such a way that human reason is far more appropriately thought of as part of this rationality instead of as the self-consciousness that knows itself over against an external totality. There is, then, another way in which a human heightening of awareness penetrates and discovers itself — not the way inward to which Augustine appealed but the way of complete self-donation to what is outside in which the seeker nevertheless finds himself. Hegel's greatness lies in fact in that he did not suppose this way of the Greeks to be a false way left behind in contrast to that modern mode of reflection, but he acknowledged that way as a facet of being itself. It was the magnificent achievement of his *Logic* to have acknowledged precisely within the dimension of the logical this ground that gathers in and underpins what points in the opposite direction. Whether he named this *nous* or God, either way it is ultimately what lies utterly outside us, just as the mystical submersion of the Christians ultimately attains inward reality.

We stand at the end of our reflections. The relationship between science and philosophy has, at the point to which Hegel (and Schelling with him) has led us, shown itself to be dialectical one. Neither the sort of philosophy that lifts itself outside the context of the sciences (which may indeed have their limited meaning), nor the speculative surpassing of limits in the direction of a dogmatic stabilization within the constant flux of research can adequately describe the relationship between philosophy and science. We need to learn to think out this relationship positively as well as in its complete polarity. There should be no slackening of the tension into "moderate Enlightenment," no "whitewashing." It would be illusory to suppose that this embarrassment would force us to place philosophy on the side of art and to give it a share in all the privileges along with the risks that are bound up with these privileges. In thinking out this relationship, we need to continue to take upon ourselves the "rigorous exertion of the concept" (*Anstrengung des Begriffs*). It is true that the claim of systematic unity appears even less redeemable today than it did in the age of Idealism. As a result an inner affinity for spellbinding multiplicity pulls upon us, which the expression of art in the riches of its works broadcasts about us. Neither the principle of self-consciousness nor any other principle of final unification and self-grounding leads us to expect to be able to go on constructing the system of philosophy. Nonetheless the exigence of reason for unity remains inexorable. Nor does this exigence stay silent before the hundred-eyed argosy that in Hegel's apt words is presented by art, in which there is not a single part that does not see us. There remains in either respect the task of self-understanding on the part of human beings with regard to themselves. This task cannot be denied in any of their experiences, surely not in the experiences of art. But just as the artistic statements become integrated with ourselves, in the process of our self-understanding, when they are perceived in their truth, it is no longer art but philosophy at work. It is the same exigence of reason, which presses us to keep on bringing about the unity of our knowledge that art too permits to enter us. To this exigence, however, there also pertains everything that the sciences afford us for taking the measure of every access to the world and probing every extent of the world. To this exigence belongs no less importantly the heritage of our tradition of philosophical reasoning, no item of which can be taken for granted and surpassed, and which we all can ill afford to let go unheeded. Reason's exigence for unity demands it.

The model of science that determines our age should also protect us from the temptation of carrying out the exigence for unity by means of precipitous constructions in our philosophizing. Just as our total experience of the world presents a process of coming to be at home that never comes to an end — to speak with Heidegger — even in a world that appears ever more strange because it has been all too changed by ourselves; so, too, the exigence for a philosophic account of things is an unending process. In it is realized not only the conversation which each of us conducts with ourselves in thinking but also the conversation in which we are all caught up together (*begriffen*) and never cease to be caught up — whether one says philosophy is dead or not.

Hegel's Philosophy and Its Aftereffects until Today

It is just as tempting as it is risky for an academic teacher to enter a circle of academically cultivated and professionally mature people not bound to him by the regular feeling connected with school classes. I would like to provide you access to a thinker whose work has become enigmatic in a rare and indeed unique measure. It is no exaggeration when I say that no living person is capable of understanding and thoughtfully reenacting the work of Hegel so that either right away or after some effort he would render completely intelligible any given passage of Hegelian statements. There is a famous story about a visit by Hegel to Goethe. Goethe, who ordinarily would have tended to lead the conversation with a certain patriarchal superiority, was extraordinarily silent at table, and Hegel, the guest, was unusually talkative, in a by all accounts peculiarly mysterious Swabian dialect. Afterward Goethe's daugher-in-law who was present at table asked when the guest had departed, "What kind of a marvelous guest was that?" And to this Goethe responded, "That was the first philosopher of Germany, Professor Hegel from Berlin." Maybe the scene will serve to remind us that Hegel belongs to the age of Goethe and that both men — equally strongly, if also in incomparable ways — left their imprint on the times that follow.

Goethe can justly be called the symbol of the bourgeois society of the nineteenth century; the man, who by reason of his talent and his brilliant personality was finally the sovereign of the Weimar court to whom the world made pilgrimage as to a prince of the mind. And on the other side, this odd Berlin professor, who in his raw Swabian way and with all the high-flown abstraction of thought that is mirrored in his works, yet managed to be the most effective teacher of philosophy in the nineteenth century. More than any of the other great thinkers, he was a figure concerning whose genuine profile the battle of the schools was waged and concerning whose true significance there was a division of opinion. After Hegel's death intellectual wars of succession raged just as following the death of a world leader. One distinguished a Hegelian right and a left. Amid the "right Hegelians" and the "left Hegelians" there raged the battle about the true content of Hegelian thought.

Among Hegel's contemporaries Goethe was surely the most universal mind, yet not even Goethe could really read Hegel. We have very good documentation for this. On the opening page of the *Phenomenology of the Spirit,* Goethe, to whom Hegel had naturally sent his book, had taken offense at a particular passage. So clearly he had started reading the book, but evidently he did not get past that first page. Completely shocked, he noted that Hegel had written something completely repugnant to him: "The bud disappears with the blooming of the blossom, and one could say that the former gets contradicted by the latter." Goethe, that convinced opponent of all revolutionary explosive theories in natural as well as human history, had, as is well known, treated the mystery of the organic growth of things precisely as the exemplar for the correct mental stance of human beings as well. Hence his repudiation of the Hegelian text. Now when one reads over that passage, one notices that if Goethe had turned the page, he would have found the passage proceeding quite in his sense with a "but . . ." that goes on to make good the organic unity. So Goethe himself did not completely realize the inner affinity that he shared with Hegel. Yet he always had a prejudice in favor of Hegel that was not a little influenced by the fact that Hegel was numbered among his defenders in the fight over Newtonian optics (being one of the proponents of Goethe's doctrine of color). It is well known that Goethe did not regard himself so much as the great poet he in fact was but as the great natural scientist who established the validity both of the true method for dealing with nature (and especially with light), and so of the true physics against Newton. The agreement of Hegel, Schelling, and Schopenhauer with Goethe's doctrine of color is, of course, not entirely without material support. It would be too facile for them to rate themselves superior physicists in the matter. What is reflected in this unhappy conflict of Goethe against Newton, however, is a phenomenon of the profoundest significance: in it is manifest that modern natural science entered the world as a truly transformative fact, and it put an end to the traditional image of science as nourished by natural observation and experience without the aid of mathematical abstraction.

Modern empirical science found its first basis in the seventeenth century in the mechanics of Galileo and Huyghens; it further unfolded and drew every area of knowledge under its methodology; and finally it sought — and this is where we currently stand — even to conquer social reality with the claim of scientific control and to take over its guidance. Fundamentally already in the seventeenth century the taken-for-granted claim of philosophy to be the *regina scientiarum,* the quintessence of all knowledge and the comprehensive framework for every possible human knowledge, was no longer plausible. Hegel was the very last to dare to defend in his thinking the proud claim of philosophy to be the framework and comprehensive totality for all possibile human knowing. To the extent that this was attempted after Hegel, it occurred within the academic horizon of the schools on the part of professors of philosophy and was no longer the world-historical reality it had been in the visage of Professor Hegel of Berlin.

Hegel attempted a final synthesis of nature and history, of nature and society, within a grandiose philosophic system of thought. Naturally because it was the last peak on the summit of the most ancient claim — of the Greek claim of thinking through the *logos* of being — it lost its popularity quite rapidly. It is characteristic of Hegel's effective history that in the year 1854, about twenty years after Hegel's death, Rudolf Heym came out with a much-discussed polemical exposition of Hegelian philosophy, and this book began with reflections upon the speedy breakdown of that philosophy. The somewhat snide, commercial tone with which Heym speaks and which, to anyone with an ear for historical tones, betrays the commercialized materialism of the early industrial development of Germany in the middle of the last century, sounded like this: "The great house only fell so quickly because this entire branch of business already lies in disarray." By this Heym means that philosophy as a whole has gone bankrupt, and the breakdown of the Hegelian domination of the world by the spirit was only a consequence of the bankruptcy of philosophy in general. And it is true: since Hegel not one thinker — perhaps one can say, not before Heidegger — has expressed the consciousness of everyone, even though his voice could be heard only *intra muros,* only within the context of the university. Of course there were great authors like Schopenhauer and Nietzsche or even Keirkegaard, but there was no longer a single philosophy teacher in the universities who really would have reached the general awareness. If today Heidegger's thought gets mocked in a novel by a novelist like Günther Grass (who does not write for experts but is widely read), this is evidence that Heidegger's voice has penetrated beyond the lecture hall.

When we ask what the reason was for the speedy demise of Hegelian philosophy, the answer is easy. The mounting up of modern research in all fields of science has discredited the claim raised and defended for the last time by Hegel of prescribing for the sciences of nature and even of integrating them within his a priori system of thought. Such a patronizing attitude on the part of the a priorism of reason had to evoke the resistance and the mockery of the empirical sciences. Today at a century's remove, we think a bit differently about the leading forces in the epoch immediately after Hegel, and we acknowledge in every field positive influences of Hegel as well. This is as true of the fundamental concepts of natural science as of the philosophy of the century that reached its peak in Neo-Kantianism, without being aware of how much Hegel lived on in it. But it is especially the so-called historical school (the movement of historical critical research centered in Berlin) that believed and knew itself in opposition to Hegel's speculative philosophy of history and about which we see today for the first time how much it was actually led by idealist philosophy and especially by Hegelian ideas.

It remains a remarkable fact that the eccentric Swabian really did not attain by extrinsic means the popularity he indeed enjoyed among his students. Incidentally this confirms a general experience that what makes a university teacher effective are not his rhetorical or formal virtues. I, for example, learned the most in the area of the history of the sciences from someone who stuttered. After a couple of hours, you do not notice the stutter anymore if the person has something to say. So maybe the Berlin students of Hegel soon did not notice any more that he spoke Swabian but took it to be German.

Nonetheless the scientific self-consciousness of the later nineteenth century was stamped by its turn away from Hegel, and this so deeply that right up to our own day Hegel has remained a suspect figure in the intellectual world internationally, especially in Anglo-Saxon countries. Today a countermovement is emerging for the first time. There are now even in England and America new Hegel societies that turn their attention again to this last thinker capable of comprehending with his philosophic genius our knowledge and our sense of the world. But all in all we have to say, today Hegel still remains suspect in the view of science and of all those who believe that all human problems are fundamentally resolvable with the progress of science.

And yet there have always been "natural" Hegelians. In Italy there was Spaventa from whom the later Italian Hegelianism known to us through the names of Croce and Gentile derives. In Holland there was a Hegel school connected with the name of Bolland, the so-called Bollandists, a group of free-thinking, liberal minds that lives on today. In England around 1900 there was a widespread Hegelianism whose traces in Oxford and Cambridge have, of course, been dissipated. And in Germany there has always been one Hegelian or another, and from such natural Hegelianism the study of Hegelian philosophy has been nurtured.

Then in 1910 Wilhelm Windelband, the head of the southwest German Neo-Kantianism, gave a speech on the new Hegelianism in the Heidelberg Academy of Sciences; in it he made himself the voice of his own students and disciples, who, within and against the dominant Neo-Kantian philosophy, had chosen to follow Hegel. One of the most vocal leaders of this Hegelianizing group was Julius Ebbinghaus, today an embittered Hegel opponent and old Kantian. But many well-known names belonged to this group — for example, Ernst Bloch, Georg von Lukács, Fedor Stepun, Richard Kroner, and Ernst Hoffmann, and a large number of young people who at that time began to invest in Hegel the highest expectations. For our own time, one would no longer be willing to claim any similar hopes. If I have been the founder and leader of an association that has devoted itself to the task of studying Hegelian philosophy, this is more with the intent of learning something from Hegel — that is, of being schooled at his level of conceptual precision and of radical energy of thought — than of renewing his perspective. This is no less true for those who say Hegel when they mean Marx. It is the things that one has to learn from Hegel that elevate Hegelianism even outside any formally organized group to a paradigm of living inquiry. I would like to show what I mean by treating three such questions: first, the religious problem of faith and knowledge; second, the problem of the objective spirit or of the historical world; and third, the question of the conceptual unity of nature and history.

The religious problem is the first in this series insofar as the partisan divisions surrounding the interpretation of Hegel went essentially back to this issue. The Hegelian right and the Hegelian left form a primarily religious division. The divisive issue was this: Is Hegel correct when he raises the claim to have comprehended even the truth of Christianity in philosophic thought and to have transposed faith into the form of knowledge; or is he — without prejudice to any personal connection with Christianity, which was not an issue in the conflict — thereby so much in the wrong that one must say that he has falsified Christian truth and helped to bring about its dissolution?

It is essential to a religion based upon true doctrine — and Christianity makes the claim of being a doctrine — that it is always beset by the suspicion of heresy. So it is that the Hegelian claim to have raised the truth of religion into the form of the philosophic concept has been particularly heavily disputed by the churches and the theological reaction. Hegel would be listed among the spiritualistic heresies that have accompanied the Christian church at least since the time of Joachim da Fiori. In these heresies the third article of the Creed, the doctrine of the Holy Spirit, would be so overemphasized that the Incarnation (God's becoming man) would basically degenerate into a continual, constantly present and ubiquitously repetitive event. In fact it is the miracle of Pentecost, the outpouring of the Holy Spirit, that keeps alive and allows to perdure that which through Christ has come into the world as the communion of saints, that is, as a community in the Spirit. In the spiritualistic heresies — and we find this in Hegel as well — the third article has always been so extremely overstressed that the death of God (the crucifixion of Jesus) and the resurrection become almost a symbol of the Spirit's ongoing power of renewal. What has been lost lives again in a new resurrection — that is, the spiritual movement by which the Spirit within humanity seeks to be raised to complete resurrection; and this transfiguration culminates in the total spiritualization of humanity and in the self-transparency of thought. While still in the form of imaginative representation, religion expounds its doctrines and interprets, for example, the sacrificial death of Jesus upon the cross as an event, as the gracious act of God; philosophic thought has raised the truth of this representation onto the conceptual level. In fact Hegel believed so, and he claimed that he had reconciled faith and knowledge. Hegel did not mean by this that no imaginative patterns of the faithful would be either possible or justified next to the clarity of thought that has comprehended itself fully. Just as little did Hegel mean by his renowned doctrine concerning the pastness of art that art no longer exists. When Hegel said, "Art is no longer the highest form of truth," he meant that what in the case of Greek sculpture still was experienced as an obvious correspondence between the divinities being honored and the visible works of art already could no longer exist with Christianity and its doctrine of the inward reality of the divine. The form of an art-religion is at an end. This means that a higher form of apprehending things, even if in the mode of imaginative representation to begin with (that is, in the form of the representations of the Christian faith), has displaced the lovely images of the gods of the ancient world.

It would be a special question for theology to take a stand in regard to Hegel's claim of having come up with a reconciliation between faith and knowledge. But there is one thing one must take seriously in any case: that religion, and precisely the Christian religion, cannot place itself in opposition to the spiritual freedom of thought of humankind without harm and that any possibility for human beings to gain insight by means of thought needs to keep itself in vital interchange with our Christian tradition and vice-versa. Hegel has defined philosophy as the thinking out of the infinite. In fact considered from the standpoint of content, that definition is an expression congruent with the imaginative representation of an infinite God and with a religion that understands the totality of the world as a creation and that believes in the vanquishing of death by the saving act of divine love.

Consequently the conflict about the Christian character of Hegelian philosophy has always flared up repeatedly. Not long ago an estimable book appeared that takes up anew the cause of the Christianness of Hegel with all the means of research worthy of philosophy: Michael Theunissen's *Hegel's Doctrine of the Absolute Spirit.*

The second point is even more effective and relevant now. It is surely the point with regard to which the indispensability of Hegel for philosophic thought is made most starkly manifest and where one can be sure that those who damn all philosophy, especially that of Hegel, actually live out of it, especially the sociologists: Hegel's doctrine of the objective spirit. The political background of this teaching has become poignantly clear since the history of Hegel's youthful years has entered into the general philosophic awareness with the publication of his youthful writings. Like his entire generation, Hegel suffered under the dissociation that reigned between the political and religious conditions of his age on the one hand and the most authentic exigencies of the spirit on the other. The great event with which the thought of German Idealism felt itself to be bound up was the French Revolution. Through it no-longer-understood forms of life and political constitution were overtaken by a new pathos of freedom. As especially Joachim Ritter has shown, that held true for Hegel as well. It is reported that even the Hegel of the Berlin period, this alleged philosopher of the Prussian state and defender of reaction, raised his glass in the midst of a circle of friends (it was, in Dresden, I believe, in the year 1823, amid the darkest period of reactionary politics under Metternich) and said, "Do you realize what day it is?" and emptied it in honor of the storming of the Bastille. So much was the French Revolution, which stands for the idea of bourgeois freedom and so the freedom of all, the leitmotif of even Hegelian thought. It lies at the basis of his philosophy of objective spirit. This doctrine of the spirit objectified in institutions is not concerned with defending the existing institutions in their unchangeable correctness. Hegel defended institutions not in a wholesale fashion but against the pretense of knowing better on the part of the individual. With his overpowering spiritual force, he showed the limitations of moralism in social life and the untenability of a purely inward morality that is not made manifest in the objective structures of life that hold human beings together. So in fact he was able to show what kind of discrepancies, not to say what sorts of injustices, as well as what kind of dialectic of unrighteousness, is connected with abstract moralism.

Hegel became a critic of Kantian moral philosophy. He criticized the extent to which this moral philosophy is perched upon moral self-certitude and thinks itself independent in its knowledge of its own duty from all external conditions, whether natural or social (especially from the system of mores and of education, the system of reward and punishment); and he was critical of the way it rests upon the notion that practical reason has the power solely in virtue of the autonomy of the self to put into effect and defend the compelling force of the moral claim against every other consideration. This Kantian impulse is great in itself, but Hegel treated it critically, especially at the point where as a morality of inwardness it amounts to a moralistic attitude over against the reality of state and society. The thrust of the theory of the objective spirit is that not the consciousness of the individual but a common and normative reality that surpasses the awareness of the individual is the foundation of our life in state and society. In grandiose fashion and chiefly in his *Phenomenology of the Spirit* and in his *Philosophy of Right* in the Berlin period, he explains the way human self-consciousness takes the decisive step toward stabilization in the recognition of its own being by the other. He develops the abstract idea of self-consciousness, which within German Idealism ultimately goes back to Descartes' *cogito me cogitare* and is raised up to the status of the fundamental principle of philosophy (in Kant it is called the I of the transcendental synthesis of apperception); and he shows that this I really undergoes an entire genesis by which it passes beyond its mere character as I into the objectivity of the spirit.

Hegel displayed the form of the I most caught up in its I-character in his discussion of sense desire. That sounds very old-fashioned. What he means is the vital feeling-for-self, the mode of being certain of oneself that occurs in sense satisfaction. This is in fact an enhancing form of self-confirmation arising

from the standpoint of our vital feeling. Here, what I am encounters itself, say, when I feel hunger. But as we know, hunger
disappears when I am full until I get hungry again, and so this
sense of self on the level of vital feeling is extremely labile.
Hegel has shown that a true sense of self is never reached by
way of this sort of subjection to and assimilation of what is alien.
Nor do I gain the least sense of self even in the structure in
which I as the master enslave others for the sake of securing
the sure satisfaction of my desires. For what can be the significance of recognition by one already dependent upon me? What
good can it do someone who seeks to discover his self-consciousness that someone else as a slave recognizes him as master? On
the contrary, it is quite another thing to be recognized by another independent self-consciousness. That bestows upon my
self-consciousness real, concrete confirmation.

We are familiar with this in terms of the phenomenon that
we broadly describe with the concept of honor. Hegel discloses
in it the dialectic of self-consciousness. It is one of the loveliest
parts of the Hegelian dialectic of thought in which one can
apprehend it in its concretization. Recognition has to be mutual.
Self-consciousness is self-consciousness only when it finds confirmation from another but in such a way that the other finds
his confirmation only from me as well. One can make this clear
by means of a simple example that everyone has experienced.
One of the most external ways of showing honor is greeting
someone. Who is not familiar with that unpleasant feeling when
one greets someone and the other indifferently looks right past
one, whether because of our having mistaken the person or
whether it is because the other does not want to acknowledge
one? To have uttered a greeting in vain is an experience in
which one's sense of self momentarily breaks down. To be sure,
greeting customs are among the most external in life. (That our
youthful generation no longer addresses us professors by title

and would rather clap us on the shoulder, as if we were Americans, does not seem to me to be an essential contribution to the reform of the academy, even though one does not necessarily need to have anything against it.) But by means of this most external of instances one can make comprehensible the more substantive aspects of our human life in common, for example, the solidarity necessary for the correct functioning of the legal system. In the critical times in which we are now living, we are quite well supplied with experiential proofs of how dangerous it is when a society is threatened in its solidarity, so that no common self-understanding supports the recognition of the legal order. One thinks, for example, of the state of perplexity that the eye witness has reached in a secularized society and that has long since given the administration of justice occasion to avoid putting witnesses under oath whenever possible. In such a situation the legal order itself has become just an external side of social reality. There are far more substantive realities of common living. Every joining together in friendship or love has such a substantive communality that may be conceptually articulated in terms of the dialectic of mutual recognition. It was one of the greatest merits of Hegel that he made the emergence of family, society, and state from this one root convincing for thought: They each arise from the overcoming and surpassing of the subjective spirit, of the individual consciousness, in the direction of a common consciousness.

I come to the third point of my considerations. Hegel, like the entire generation of his time, was moved forward along the path of his thought by a fundamental experience, and that was the experience of alienation. He named it *positivity* (*Positivität*). With Hegel one has to become accustomed to the way he often means by an expression just about the opposite of what one would expect. So when Hegel says positivity, he means something quite negative: that norms have been imposed solely as outwardly authoritative and have not been inwardly affirmed by ourselves. It would be an instance of the positivity in Christianity that it requires sheer obedience of the faithful, even without any taint of insight or inner engagement. It would be an instance of the positivity of a constitution when it carries on as valid in its positive determinations, though there is not any living spirit in it. As we know it was the legal setup of the Roman Empire in the German nation that provided Hegel in his youth with a vivid field of perception for just such a decline, with the dissociation between the externally and positively valid and the factually real. One is reminded that the end of the Roman Empire of the German nation was basically drawn out in endless trials, in Regensburg or elsewhere, while the essential element of a genuine imperial constitution, to provide an order for the genuine solidarity of all Germans, had become ineffective and lifeless on account of the modern territorial state, the confessional oppositions, and the conflicts among absolutist principalities.

Alienation, this primary point of departure of Hegel, entails as its correlative the reconciliation of alienation or also, as he phrases it, "the reconciliation of corruption." That is the task Hegel had set himself as a thinker: reestablishing the reconciliation of all alienations through the power of philosophic thought. To resume my first point, quite early on Hegel obviously was sensitive to the fact that the notion of reconciliation is an authentic form of the Christian message. We possess an essay by Hegel's comrade in school, Hölderlin, on the theme, "Jesus as the Genius of Reconciliation." This is a theme of the Enlightenment and anything but a matter of theological orthodoxy. We would say that this is something Harnack or some other liberal theologian at the end of the nineteenth century could have said. It is not the theological element that is important here but that reconciliability or reconciliation has been shown by Hegel to be an authentic phenomenon of human spirituality. It resides in the dialectic of self-consciousness as well.

There is no friendship, no marriage, no relationship of love in which the inner sense of mutual trust between human beings does not grow through conflict and reconciliation. This mystery of reconciliation is the secret of Hegelian dialectic. It is called synthesis. If one wants to determine by what means Hegel has become the conclusive figure of the great tradition of metaphysical philosophy and what it is that makes him stand out in the great series of this tradition, then I would say, he expanded the grand conception of Greek metaphysics on a modern footing with the completely different hemisphere presented by the historical realm. The magnificence of Greek metaphysics was that it sought reason in the cosmos; it sought the *nous,* which is at work ordering and distinguishing in all the formations of nature. To see reason in nature, that was the Greek heritage. Hegel had tried to show reason in history as well. At first this would appear to be a surdlike paradox — not only in our view but also in the view of Hegel's own time — to assert that in reckoning the buzzing confusion of human affairs by the calm courses pursued by the stars in heaven, the comparison really stands up. That had been in fact the model for Greek cosmology and metaphysics: the order of the solar system, which had already been recognized by the Pythagoreans as a mathematically and musically determined harmony. That in the confusion of human affairs, in this up and down of inconsistency, nothing lasting could maintain itself was familiar to the eighteenth century, especially in view of the example of the decline of the ecumenic empire of Rome. The great writers of history and philosophers of history of the eighteenth century were almost fixated upon the theme of how the antique *oikumene* collapsed.

That in human history a reasonableness should perdure and make itself manifest similar to that in nature was the bold thesis.

The renowned phrase he had formulated in the preface to the *Philosophy of Right,* which tends to release the joking of all who do not wish to bother with thought, implies that thesis: "What is rational is real, and what is real is rational." At first one will find this an impossible assertion. Can one deliver oneself over in this way with bound hands to an aging reality and find all that exists is good? But is that what is intended? By "reality" does Hegel really mean what we understand upon first construing this statement? Does he not actually mean — and it is utterly plain that he does mean this — that in the long run the irrational is not capable of really lasting? Is it so perverse to think that in reality the irrational cannot hold out in the long run? And is it not just the overwhelming phenomenon of our historical experience of ourselves that the individual with his plans, action, hopes, disappointments, and desperations is active and alive without really knowing in the end what he is accomplishing and doing with respect to history as a whole and for society as a whole? It is precisely our experience of history that we are located so completely within it that we can in a certain sense always say, We don't know what is happening to us. History consists precisely of the fact that we do not realize what is happening to us and that nevertheless we are involved in this play, each one in his place or — as the younger people are so particularly sensitive to — each one looking for and not finding a place from which one could actively and transformatively work on a bad reality. So I think Hegel's statement, "What is rational is real, and what is real is rational," articulates a task for each individual rather than a legitimation for the inactivity of us all.

Intimately connected with this thought perhaps is one of the most prophetic insights of Hegel. We know that Hegel had applied a three-step dialectic of thesis-antithesis-synthesis to world history. He read history as a progress of freedom. If in the Orient one was free and all others unfree; and in Greece only those who were citizens of a city were free while the others were slaves; so in the end it is through Christianity and modern history, especially the emancipation of the third estate and the liberation of the peasants, that we have arrived at the point where all are free. Therefore has the end of history come about? Can there still be history in Hegel's view once the freedom of all has come to light? And just what has become of history since then? As a matter of fact, since then history is not to be based upon a new principle. The principle of freedom is unimpugnable and irrevocable. It is no longer possible for anyone still to affirm the unfreedom of humanity. The principle that all are free never again can be shaken. But does this mean that on account of this, history has come to an end? Are all human beings actually free? Has not history since then been a matter of just this, that the historical conduct of man has to translate the principle of freedom into reality? Obviously this points to the unending march of world history into the openness of its future tasks and gives no becalming assurance that everything is already in order.

The Heritage of Hegel

No one should take upon himself the task of measuring all that has come down to us in the great heritage of Hegelian thought. It ought to be enough for each person to be the heritage himself and to give an account of what he has received from this inheritance. But least of all can someone undertake to evaluate this heritage whose own contribution to philosophic thought lies decades in the past; and to do so for the younger generations who have entered upon this heritage on their own and who confirm the limits of his competence precisely by the fact that they value his merits. Moreover no one should imagine himself able to reap the harvest of an entire epoch or indeed even merely to assess it. Even Hegel himself did not do this — Hegel whom overzealous epigones want to burden with the notion that the idea he thought through and named "absolute knowledge" comprised the actual end of history. Hegel knew better when he — ultimately to be sure in regard to himself as well — cited the following: "See the feet of those who are going to take you away are already standing in front of the door."[1]

So instead of delivering a pretentious contribution to scholarly research or a comprehensive report on the state of research in the field, allow me simply to narrate how in my opinion the heritage of Hegel has been transposed in my own attempts at thought.

The philosophic turn, which I, in connection with impulses from the thought of Heidegger, have tried to give to the Romantic hermeneutics and its progressive development by way of the historical school through Ranke, Droysen, Dilthey, and his disciples, is inseparable from the all-encompassing synthesis of Hegel.[2] Here for the first time the notion of the *logos* that the Greeks had worked out for the apprehension of the world in its totality was extended to the historical world without assuming the suprarational data of a salvation history. To come to know reason in history was Hegel's bold claim, and in the end it drew upon itself just as much resistance as his attempt — long since antiquated and doomed to fail from the outset — to bend the modern investigation of nature, in spite of its essentially provisional character and its way of constantly overtaking itself, under the concept of a science that would be a totality of truth (*doctrina*), that is, which affirmed an absolute, rational truth. In the end, the dialectic of absolute knowledge — in the domain of the historical spirit — had just as little chance of escaping the resistance of historical research. It could hardly avoid following a path very similar to that traveled by the idealist philosophy of nature through the victorious course of the scientific investigation of nature. The open dialectic of the Platonist, Schleiermacher, must have appeared far more promising as the foundation for a methodology of the historical sciences than Hegel's construction of world history. And so Dilthey, Schleiermacher's biographer, and the methodology of the historical school of which Dilthey was the philosophical interpreter, undertook an epistemological grounding of the *Geisteswissenschaften* under the motto of hermeneutics. But it was within philosophy itself that Hegel's conceptual achievement, the speculative method of dialectics, met with sharpest resistance.[3] For it is of a sort that before it one's understanding literally stands silent, full of astonishment and protest. This came about in the Neo-Kantianism that was having an ever greater influence. Its slogan, "Back to Kant," referred not least to the speculative hubris of absolute Idealism; from a Kantian basis and in dependence upon Lotze, it proposed in its turn the critical grounding of the *Geisteswissenschaften* upon the concept of value.[4]

Be that as it may, Hegel's legacy and especially the notion of the objective spirit ultimately gained renewed power over Dilthey and even over Neo-Kantianism and the phenomenology that was emerging in our century. Here was a way indicated of overcoming the one-sidedness of modern subjectivism and especially that of the "psychological" interpretation, which Schleiermacher's genial gift for empathy not only added to the traditional methods of the theory of interpretation but singled out for special distinction. The theory of objective spirit became the most effective heritage of Dilthey's school (Spranger, Litt, Freyer, E. Rothacker) and of Neo-Kantianism just as it was going into dissolution (E. Lask, E. Cassirer, N. Hartmann).[5] And so it remained for me to decide — between the alternatives of the "psychological reconstruction of past thought" and the "integration of past thought into one's own thought" — against Schleiermacher and in favor of Hegel.[6] To be sure, Hegel's *Philosophy of World History* remained caught in the insoluble contradiction of an open progress of history and a conclusive apprehension of its meaning, and it could not be repeated if one were intent on taking historicity seriously.

In this way I became an advocate of the "bad infinite" for which the end keeps on delaying its arrival — something that for Hegel is not merely an untruth but a truth as well. In particular the philosophical energy with which Martin Heidegger had set up the paradox of a hermeneutics of facticity as a counterpoise to the transcendental phenomenology of Husserl and his program of a new science of consciousness inspired me.[7]

That precisely the unilluminable obscurity of our facticity —
what Heidegger called "thrownness" (*Geworfenheit*) — sustains
and does not merely set limits to the project character of human
Dasein, had to bestow a new weight on the historicity of human
Dasein and on the significance of history for our *Dasein.* Our
understanding of history is not only a question of acquiring
knowledge and familiarity or of the development of the historical sense; it is also a matter of the shaping of our destiny. That
understanding is not so much an act of consciousness as something that one comes up against in which the historical richness
of the spirit builds up; that understanding also and above all is
a happening and makes history. It was heresy to assert these
things over against Husserl's program of philosophy as a rigorous science, with its grounding in the apodictic certitude of
the self-consciousness. In truth, however, the thinking out of
the historicity of *Dasein* was just as little capable of being written
off by Husserl as historicism and relativism as Dilthey's "Construction of the Historical World in the Geisteswissenschaften."
One could learn this from Heidegger. Heidegger's turn toward
the hermeneutics of facticity was a turn away from the Idealism
that stresses consciousness in the Neo-Kantian mold from which
Husserl too was cast; however, it was not relativism but a philosophic counterproject. It included an ontological critique of the
notions of objectivity and subjectivity, which had remote origins
in the beginnings of Greek thought, so it was redolent precisely
of Hegel's critique of extrinsic reflection when Heidegger distinguished the ontological dimension of questioning from every
ontic question. Especially when Heidegger, in the development
of his thinking, toned down the existential pathos of his great
pioneering work and came to acknowledge his own transcendental self-understanding as inadequate, it came ever more
starkly to light that Hegel's doctrine of the objective spirit had
not exhausted its real relevance. When one reflects today upon

the thoughtworthy discussion that Ernst Cassirer (who had further developed Neo-Kantian Idealism in the direction of the *Philosophy of Symbolic Form*) held in 1930 with the young Martin Heidegger in Davos, one realizes clearly how Hegel's heritage lived on in both thinkers and how the younger of the two should have felt himself compelled to a lifelong dialogue with Hegel.

It may be shown that Hegel's "reflection in itself" represents a figure of thought in which an Aristotelian legacy predominated and was renewed and which at the same time was not utterly remote from Heidegger's thought, which had been nourished upon the critique of Greek ontology. Being (*Das Sein*) as "being true" (*Wahrsein*), the self-presentation of coming-to-presence (*Wesens*), that one calls "thinking"; this was the central motif that inspirited Heidegger's early interpretations of Aristotle (which have never been published).[8] The emphasis placed by the young Heidegger upon the way disclosure (*Aletheia*) does not have its primordial place in propositions (*Sätze*) but in being (*Sein*) was a prelude to the later Heidegger's turn away from transcendental self-interpretation; and it prepared that thinking upon being (*Sein*), which as the lighting process (*Lichtung*) of being, as the being (*Sein*) of the lighting process is the "there" (*Da*) that opens upon its own and antecedes every possible self-manifestation by any entity.[9] In any case, the well-honed metaphors in which Heidegger later attempted to speak about being (*Sein*) that is not the being of any entity (*Seiendem*), *Differenz, Lichtung, Ereignis,* came far closer to the speculative dialectic of Hegelian concepts than the academic Neo-Hegelianism that had been worked out within the framework of Neo-Kantianism, especially in the Heidelberg of the day, managed to do.

Then, too, one should not fail to note that the motives that compelled Heidegger to his so-called *Kehre* ("turnabout") harmonized with a new sensibility or style of the epoch, which,

exhausted from the subtle sensuality of impressionistic enchant-
ment, called out for a new, constructive objectivity. Already in
1907 Richard Hamann, one of the teachers of my youthful
years after 1918, had concluded the laying to rest of impres-
sionism in life and art with the demand, "More Hegel." It is
known that Hegel found a lasting home in other lands, for
instance in Italy, and that the constructive spirit of modern art
in our century had hurried far ahead of the German development. Van Gogh and Cezanne and a generation later Juan Gris
and Picasso, for example, became symbolic representatives of a
new outburst, which then enveloped the German scene. It was
similar in literature, where Mallarmé's *poesie pure* represents the
poetic correlate of Hegel's absolute knowledge, and in German
literature the discovery of the late Hölderlin, as well as George's
formally stringent art of versifying and Rilke's thing-poems
(*Dinggedichte*). These were developments that helped to promote
the language of poetry as well as that of thought to a new
objective power of symbolization. It is no accident that the earliest documentation of the *Kehre* in Heidegger's thought reached
verbal expression in his Hölderlin lecture in Rome in 1936 and
that in other ways as well the old Romantic neighborliness of
poetry and philosophy came to new life. These things had made
a great impression upon me from very early on.

It is true that Heidegger at that time no longer trusted the
notion of hermeneutics to keep his thinking free from the consequences of a transcendental theory of consciousness, just as
he tried mightily to overcome the language of metaphysics by
means of a special half-poetic language.[10] But to me, it seemed,
fell precisely the task of speaking on behalf of the happening
that resides in understanding and of the overcoming of modern
subjectivism in an analysis of the hermeneutic experience that
has become reflectively aware of itself. So already in 1934 I

began with a critical analysis of aesthetic consciousness, concerning which I sought to prove[11] that it did not do justice to the truth claim of art; and accompanied by a constant intercourse with the Greek classics, especially with Plato, I sought to overcome the historical self-estrangement with which historical positivism deflated ideas into opinions and philosophy into doxography.[12] I was helped by the theory of contemporaneity that Kierkegaard, for religious and critical theological reasons, had set up against "understanding at a distance" and that attained in 1924 a persuasive effectiveness through the Diederich edition of the "religious discourses" (*Life and Rule of Love*). Already, however, one of my earliest experiences in thought — by way of a detour through Kierkegaard, together with a paradoxical enthusiasm for the assessor, William, in *Either/Or* — had led me to Hegel, without my completely having realized it.

To be sure, what so formed my thinking was a personalized, dialogical Hegel behind whom there always stood the daily, thoughtful intercourse with the Platonic dialogues. Over and above this, from very early on I had sought to maintain a critical distance toward the academic aridities of *Kathederphilosophie* that I encountered in a series of experiences with my own teachers. Life experience and the study of Plato had led me quite early to the insight that the truth of a single proposition cannot be measured by its merely factual relationship of correctness and congruency; nor does it depend merely upon the context in which it stands. Ultimately it depends upon the genuineness of its enrootedness and bond with the person of the speaker in whom it wins its truth potential, for the meaning of a statement is not exhausted in what is stated. It can be disclosed only if one traces its history of motivation and looks ahead to its implications. From that time forward this became one of my guiding hermeneutical insights. Here the heritage of Dilthey flowed together with the phenomenological clarification brought about by Husserl. Why, in our view, does Socrates, even though he often brings about the downfall of the most reasonable, the most Socratic, responses of his interlocutors with the most questionable logical means, remain free from the suspicion of being merely one of these negative Sophists who play out the game of their dialectical superiority?[13] All due honor to "logic," but the smiling superiority with which the Platonic arguments are examined as to their logical validity in modern research — and at best are even improved upon in a well-meaning way — always appeared to me to be an almost comic *metabasis eis allo genos*. It is a confusion of the scientific procedures of proof for the persuasive power of dialogue, of logic for the rhetoric of thought whose old name was "dialectic." But I would have to spend long years still before the central position of the dialogue in the theory of hermeneutics and for the linguistic character of our experience of world as a whole made its way into my thought.

For that to occur, help was needed from many sides. One sort came to me at the time of the World War II by way of the autobiography of Collingwood, the disciple of B. Croce and the last representative of English Hegelianism.[14] There I found exactly what I was well accustomed to in my philological and interpretive practice, made perceptible in masterly fashion in relation to the research experience of the great discoverer of the boundary walls in Roman Britain and raised up to the status of a principle as "the logic of question and answer." Just as Collingwood had illuminated the course of the Roman *limes* not by the accident of a lucky archeological discovery but by virtue of the prior posing and answering of the question how such a protective device reasonably would have had to be set up, so too the intercourse with the philosophic tradition becomes meaningful only when reason is recognized in it. This means that reason directs its own questions to it. That one only "understands" a statement when one understands it as an answer to a question is compellingly evident. That I nonetheless could not completely follow the theory of historical knowledge, the theory of reenactment, constructed by Collingwood was due to his misleading confusion (which often bedevils contemporary thought about these matters) of practice and action, through which the essence and experience of history is voluntaristically distorted. A theory of planning or of action can never do justice to the experience of history in which our plans tend to shatter and our actions and omissions tend to lead to unexpected consequences.

But such short-circuited applications that I found in Collingwood did not basically deter me: I had come to know the stronger position of Hegel that lay behind it, to be sure in an undogmatic, free fashion. That the consciousness of the individual — prescinding from the exceptional case of "world-historical individuals" — is no match for reason in history Hegel had illuminatingly demonstrated in his famous doctrine about the cunning of reason (*List der Vernunft*). But must not this knowledge of the finitude and limitedness of the individual who stands as an agent in history affect any individual who thinks? What must this mean for the claim of philosophic thought to truth? That the old form of the proposition is not suitable for expressing speculative truths Hegel had indeed both known and told us; but this insight needs to be turned against himself and the methodological compulsion to which he was subject. What convinced me about Collingwood's logic of question and answer was not its methodological usefulness, which is ultimately trivial, but its validity (that transcends all methodical usage) according to which question and answer are utterly entangled with one another. For what then is a question? Surely something that one has to understand and that one does understand only when one understands the question itself in terms of something, that is, as an answer; and in doing so one limits the dogmatic claim of any proposition. The logic of question and answer proved itself a dialectic of question and answer in which question and answer are constantly exchanged and are dissolved in the movement of understanding.

Thus there emerged all at once and behind all methodology of the *Geisteswissenschaften* and all epistemology the unity of dialogue and dialectic that related Hegel and Plato to one another in a surprising manner, and this set the hermeneutic experience free. It was no longer confined to the "being-toward-a-text," to the procedure for interrogating and construing pre-given texts by the methodically informed interpreter. Suddenly the motivating interest that antecedes all knowledge and interpretation, the mystery of the question, took the center. A question arises; it imposes itself; it is indemonstrable. It is not hard to realize that there is no method for learning how to ask questions, and one recalls that the old piece of rhetorical doctrine, *de inventione,* contains at least an indirect indication of the significance of the question for all knowledge. The structure of the dialogue should prove itself a key for the role that linguisticality (*Sprachlichkeit*) plays for all coming to know and understanding.

At the same time, however, another, greater teacher was brought to my attention. I mean Aristotle, who had first been opened up to me, a quite young man myself, by the young Heidegger. In relation to the Aristotelian theory of *phronesis,* of practical rationality, I had begun to learn how to clarify conceptually the pathos of *Existenzphilosophie* typical of the reception accorded Kierkegaard at the time. What Kierkegaard had taught us and what we then called "existential" (*existenziell*) (decades before "existentialism" was formulated in France), found its prototype in the unity of *ethos* and *logos* that Aristotle had thematized as practical philosophy, and especially as the virtue of practical rationality. To be sure, the two-thousand-year tradition of practical philosophy that goes back to Aristotle ultimately fell prey to the pressure of the modern notion of science. The turn from "politics" as a discipline of "practical philosophy," still cultivated especially by historians until late in the nineteenth century, to *Politologie* (in German parlance) or "political science," is a telling expression of this. But there remains to the former a moment that offers an exact correspondence to the hermeneutic experience, and especially to that operative in the sciences. Whoever possesses the virtue of practical rationality is aware of the normative viewpoints he follows and knows how to make them effective in the concrete decision demanded by the practical situation.

One is aware, then, of the normative viewpoints in the practical situation in which one stands, but not in the sense of theoretic knowledge, but owing to its binding validity. Practical philosophy in its turn can make this awareness an object of its theory, as Aristotle, say, describes the "ethical virtues" in outline. But the theoretician can only see these viewpoints adequately, from the standpoint of their fulfilled concretization, insofar as he experiences himself as bound by their validity. This is the way Aristotle restricted the possibilities of theoretical insight in the practical field. Now it seems to me that the same holds true for hermeneutics and hence for the *Geisteswissenschaften,* and for all understanding in general.[15] The practice of understanding, in life as in science, is similarly the expression of the affinity of the one who understands to the one whom he understands and to that which he understands. The theoretical giving-an-account of the possibilities of understanding is not an objectifying reflection that makes understanding something capable of being mastered by means of science and methodology. It shows forth instead that the universal as something of which one is aware is subject to the indissoluble problematic of its rational application.

But thereby the problem of hermeneutics proves to be a fundamental problem of philosophy in general. Like practical philosophy, philosophical hermeneutics stands beyond the alternatives of transcendental reflection and empirical-pragmatic knowledge. In the end it was the great theme of the concretization of the universal that I learned to think of as the basic experience of hermeneutics, and so I entered once again the neighborhood of the great teacher of concrete universality, Hegel. Not only theology and jurisprudence were and are at all times familiar with the hermeneutical task of concretizing the universal from time immemorial. That the universality of the rule is in need of application and that for the application of rules there exists in turn no rule, one could have been able to learn from Kant's *Critique of Judgment* and from its successors, especially from Hegel, if not from one's own insight.

We stand full of wonder before Hegel's grand synthesis of Christianity and philosophy, of nature and spirit, of Greek metaphysics and transcendental philosophy, which he projected in the guise of absolute knowledge. But it is not completely relevant for us. The century and a half that separates us from Hegel may not be gainsaid. I would not want to see in Hegel himself the destruction of "the certain foundation of transcendental consciousness, in terms of which the a priori drawing of boundaries between transcendental and empirical determinations, between validity and genesis, appeared to be certain," as Habermas once formulated it; but that the overwhelming power of his synthesis worked in this direction; and that we have experienced this effect throughout an entire century, which one names the historical century, is certain. Marx, Nietzsche, and Freud exposed the limits of the self-certitude of thought thinking itself.

So there is no question of Hegel discipleship, but of interiorizing the challenge that he represents. Under this challenge, the basic experience of hermeneutics began to reveal its true universality inasmuch as our use of language, or better, inasmuch as the use that language finds in us whenever we think, pervades our whole experience of the world. It is constantly achieving the concretization of the universal.[16] Thus hermeneutics had traded its service function, which it had possessed as the methodology of the *Geisteswissenschaften,* for an all-determining position; it had become philosophy. The tendencies of our century that I shared in by thinking about language as the true concretization of the universal converge everywhere with the Platonic-Aristotelian heritage of Greek dialectic, which was always my special interest in scholarly research. But they also preserve something of the grand synthesis of reason and history risked by Hegel, even though they are not aware of this. In the linguistic character of our access to the world, we are implanted in a process of tradition that marks us as historical in essence. Language is not an instrumental setup, a tool, that we apply, but the element in which we live and which we can never objectify to the extent that it ceases to surround us.

This element that surrounds us nevertheless is nothing like an enclosure from which we could ever strive to escape. The element of language is not a mere empty medium in which one thing or another may be encountered. It is the quintessence of everything that can encounter us at all. What surrounds us is language as what has been spoken, the universes of discourse (*ta legomena*). To dwell in language means to be moved in speaking about something and in speaking to someone. Even when we speak a foreign language, it is not language that surrounds us so much as what is spoken in it. But since it surrounds us as what is spoken and not as the threatening field of otherness in relation to which there can only be self-affirmation, conquest, or submission, it gives shape to the space of our freedom.

Even though the idealism of freedom developed by Hegel and his generation appears abstract, even though today the freedom of everyone that Hegel designated as the goal of world history appears utopian in the face of the mounting lack of freedom of all, and even though the contradiction between what is real and what would be rational is ultimately indissoluble — all this testifies to our freedom. Neither natural necessities nor causal compulsions determine our thinking and our intending — whether we will and act, fear or hope or despair, we are moved in the space of freedom. This space is not the free space of an abstract joy in construction but a space filled with reality by prior familiarity.

For this Hegel had the beautiful expression "making oneself at home." Being at home in no way includes becoming partisan for what has already been passed down. Just as much it grounds the freedom for criticism and for projecting new goals in social life and action. Precisely therein does it make sense to confess oneself an heir of Hegel — not by thinking of his anticipation of the absolute as a knowledge that we entrust to philosophy; still less by expecting philosophy to serve the demands of the day and to legitimate itself before any authority that pretends to know what the moment requires. It suffices to acknowledge with Hegel the dialectic of the universal and concrete as the summation of the whole of metaphysics until now and along with this to realize that this has to be summed up ever anew. Indeed one talks about the end of metaphysics and about the scientific age in which we stand, and perhaps even about the lack of history proper to the technological age we are now entering. In the end, Hegel could turn out to be right. We would, of course, be in the position of saying of humanity as a whole what Hegel had said about "a cultured people": that without metaphysics it would be "like a temple without the holy of holies."[17]

The condition of having been set outside the grooves of naturalness that distinguishes us as thinking beings everywhere and ever again strikes against the limits beyond which our thinking is nonetheless irresistibly driven. By means of science, by means of the "big bang," there comes to life for every man today the enigma of the beginning, to which the theology of creation once offered its answer — or was it a question? — the enigma of the universe, which took its earliest conceptual form in the *logos* of the cosmos and which gets ever more deeply revealed in the expanding universe of nature and of history; the enigma of human freedom, as well as of human reason, which we have to keep on doubting on the basis of our experience and yet to which as thinking beings we necessarily have to lay claim again; and finally there is the thinking out of finitude, the thinking through of the end of ourselves as thinking beings, an idea of which thinking itself can hardly lay hold. All of this does not let us go. The ancient Greek, "Know thyself!" still holds good for us as well, for it meant, "Know that you are no god, but a human being." What self-knowledge really is is not the perfect self-transparency of knowledge but the insight that we have to accept the limits posed for finite natures. But just as the great Greek thinkers still could not follow the admonition to humility, which especially their poets tended to raise, but surrendered themselves to the drive toward questioning for the sake of "becoming immortal as far as possible,"[18] so, too, Hegel's heritage will not let us free.

That does not mean that metaphysics as a science, this unique form (*Gestalt*) of our Western civilization that found in Hegel its triumphal completion and its end, would be possible for us. But without this heritage of metaphysics, it would not be possible for us even to comprehend what that science is that determines our age most profoundly, and what place it assumes and what function it serves within our own self-understanding. In full awareness of our finitude we remain exposed to questions that go beyond us. They befall us — if not already the individual in his most quiet moments, then all of us from the vantage of that in the light of which we all know ourselves; and in this way we all confirm Hegel's doctrine of the absolute spirit. With him we know about the manifoldness of the encounter with ourselves that reaches beyond every historical conditionedness. We encounter ourselves in art, in spite of all social utilitarianism. We encounter ourselves in the challenge of religion that perdures in the age of science. No less do we encounter ourselves in thinking. There it is the questions that we call philosophical and that promote us ever further in our intercourse with our philosophic tradition. From them in truth no thinking being can ever completely hold himself at a remove. I do not need to demonstrate this further in Swabian country. These questions hold us in suspense.

Afterword

My Hegel speech, with which I thanked the city of Stuttgart for the distinction I received, tries to present the tension-filled proximity that the development of a philosophical hermeneutics manifests in relation to the magnificent thought project of Hegel. Even if one would like to regard the final form of speculative Idealism as the conclusive systematic foundation of philosophy, after a century and a half one cannot simply wish to barricade oneself in the house of this thought. At the start of our century Benedetto Croce had sensed the same need for discriminating the living and the dead in Hegel's philosophy and so to draw a sum from the advancing tradition of Italian

Hegelianism. Something similar took place in England (by McTaggart and Bradley) and in Holland (by Bolland). At just about the same time in Germany there set in a renewed approach to the philosophy of Hegel, departing from the Neo-Kantianism that then dominated the academic scene and was beginning to near its end. Windelband lent this movement his voice in his address to the Heidelberg Academy of Sciences of 1910, and the new movement was carried along by the circle of his disciples, by Emil Lask and Richard Kroner, by Julius Ebbinghaus, Georg von Lukács, and Ernst Bloch, as well as many others. But only when the whole mass of the Romantic heritage of the *Geisteswissenschaften* poured into Neo-Kantianism's transcendental philosophic continuation, which once again repeated the journey from Kant to Hegel, was the consciousness of the epoch as a whole embraced anew by the philosophic thought of Hegel.

That meant in truth that Hegel himself was liberated from his thin-blooded academic repristinization and placed back in the context of his most characteristic motifs. The epochal awareness of the early twentieth century came increasingly under the influence of Friedrich Nietzsche and the philosophy of life, which found in Henri Bergson its leading European spokesman. The novelty was that one questioned behind the statements of self-consciousness, and in the name of historical consciousness, of the critique of ideology, and of depth psychology disputed the truth claims of philosophy as grounded upon the notion of transcendental subjectivity and the unshakableness of self-consciousness. In this situation, the new familiarity with Hegel's early political-theological sketches, which had been edited by Hermann Nohl at the urging of Wilhelm Dilthey, found a strong resonance and opened up new perspectives. It was the new concretization that the Idealist principle of self-consciousness had gained in Hegel that now became visible in his regard.

From the notion of life, which was derived from Schelling as the potency of the organism, and upon which was grounded the higher potency of self-consciousness, after it had been burst open by the "lightning flash from the absolute," but especially from the Johannine notion of love, which the young Hegel had thematized in its religious and social facets, the total horizon broadened out in which the thinking of Hegel appeared.

Herbert Marcuse's dissertation, written under Heidegger, is symptomatic of this.[19] It centers on the inner interweaving of life, consciousness, and spirit or mind. And so what Heidegger had in view in his questioning behind the "fantastically idealized subject" of transcendental philosophy could lead to a certain proximity with Hegel. A Neo-Kantian and logician basing his thought on "the fact of science" in the style of Cohen or a phenomenologist of transcendental subjectivity in the style of Husserl was, at any rate, no Hegel. And so, from early on,[20] Heidegger experienced the attraction from Hegel's side — and precisely for that reason pursued his critical delimitation over against Hegel. Hegel, going beyond "subjective Idealism," was close enough to him to challenge him all the more.[21]

For Heidegger and for his students it had to be a constant preoccupation to determine the proximity to and distance from Hegel. If I should come before the public with my report on the heritage of Hegel and on what I have developed as hermeneutical philosophy, I ought to take up the question as to how I can believe hermeneutics avoids the consequences drawn by Hegel when he traced out in a comprehensive analysis the necessary course of the spirit through the forms of consciousness in which it appeared. In an essay in his *Holzwege*, Heidegger entered so deeply into the path of the argument of the *Phenomenology of the Spirit* that the resistance of his own thinking in doing so was almost unnoticeable. I have made some contributions to the question regarding the ambivalence of Heidegger's stance toward Hegel;[22] and I have tried to bring the lasting heritage of Hegel to bear and especially to purify the dialectic of self-consciousness from short-circuited applications (by Marx, by Kojève, and by Sartre).[23] But the challenge remains that Heidegger took up the critical motifs of Schelling, Kierkegaard, and Nietzsche and from the standpoint of the basic hermeneutic constitution of *Dasein* drew into his critical destruction of metaphysics the idea of absolute knowledge, as well as the mutual reflection of Christian religion and absolute spirit hazarded by Hegel's universal synthesis.

The hermeneutics I developed was also based upon finitude and the historical character of *Dasein,* and it tried to carry forward Heidegger's turn away from his transcendental account of himself, albeit not in Heidegger's direction of an inspiration from the poetic *mythos* of Hölderlin but rather in a return to the open dialectic of Plato and in reliance upon that "dampening down of subjectivity," as Julius Stenzel called it, that from early on had attracted me toward Greek thought. It was only consistent then that just as in the thought of our century as a whole, so too in hermeneutics the problem of language came more and more into the foreground; and the occurrence of language in understanding and agreement became the underpinning of finitude. It corresponded with the intention of Heidegger's thought to the degree that he knew himself to be *unterwegs zur Sprache* ("on the way to language"). To be sure I had good reasons for placing the dialogical character of language in the foreground. Not only was the centering in the subjectivity of self-consciousness thereby overcome, but above all I strove in this way to support the struggle led by Heidegger in his almost tragic grappling against a fall back into the language of metaphysics.

In my contributions to the Löwith festschrift, I had already tried to overcome Heidegger's perspective according to which we do not get out of the language of metaphysics because the grammar of our languages binds our thought to it by means of a consideration in the opposite direction.[24] Figures of speech, parables, and all the other indirect modes of speech that have been developed in the Near and Far East exhibit a narrative structure and still mediate insights of philosophic metaphysics. The language of these texts has nothing to do with the predicative structure of the judgment and is independent of any determinate grammar. Even in translation such discourses and proverbs maintain a profound intelligibility.

On the other hand, Heidegger's half-poetic attempts at discourse are sometimes more expressive of a linguistic need than of its overcoming. So I have pointed toward the interchange of dialogue and to the dialogical structure of language in which an entirely undogmatic dialectic is constantly enacted, and I have shown the way a communal language is shaped in it beyond the explicit awareness of the individual speaker and how a step-by-step unveiling of being comes about in this way. This, however, is repeated in the conversation of the soul with itself, which since Plato is the way we think of thinking. Certainly such a disclosure of being occurs in an utterly different, immediate manner in a fully achieved poem; and so we call a poem in which this is missing empty. The dialogical structure of thinking can never attain such immediacy, but it can be moved toward it. That is the dimension of the hermeneutical experience. Even in Hegel's speculative displacement of the proposition, the effort of conceptualization seeks to overcome the deformation of thought into a substantialist metaphysics that is embedded in the very form of the judgment and of the proposition, and to express speculative truths.

Thus the dialogical structure of all understanding and all agreement that I elaborated has proven to be of such universal relevance that our relationship to tradition and especially to the thought history of Western metaphysics is also modified by it. What appears in Heidegger's perspective as a growing oblivion of being nonetheless makes a case for his partnership in the conversation of thought with itself.[25] The extreme consequences of thought heightened by Nietzsche with anguished enthusiasm and by Heidegger with eschatological pathos found a counterpoise in the continuity of a linguistically interpreted order of life that is constantly being built up and renewed in family, society, and state.

To emphasize this as I did in *Truth and Method* may sound like blind optimism in an age of faith in science and of the flattening technological destruction of all that has flourished. In fact, behind this optimism stands a profound skepticism regarding the role of "intellectuals" and especially of philosophy in humanity's household of life. Not that I would deny the ubiquity of philosophy. I am even convinced of the fact that there are no people who do not "think" sometime and somewhere. That means there is no one who does not form general views about life and death, about freedom and human living together, about the good and about happiness. These views usually rest upon unacknowledged biases and short-circuited generalizations, and perhaps one can say that in the attempts at thought and conceptual clarifications of the "philosopher" they find their criticism and to that extent a certain legitimation, at least for the one who thinks further. But that is the most that can be expected of it. The great equilibrium of what is living, which sustains and permeates the individual in his privacy as well as in his social constitution and in his view of life, also encompasses those who think. Nietzsche may have formulated this truth a bit too provocatively when he spoke of the "little reason" of human beings. More serene was the Greek thought that held the raising to clarity of knowledge and the happiness of *theoria* to be the supreme form of human life and acknowledged it as the ideal of the best life; but it also knew that such theory is embedded within the practice of conditioned and lived life and is borne along by it.[26]

So there was a material reason why, in thinking through the hermeneutic phenomenon, I was directed more and more toward the model of Aristotle's practical philosophy. In his Kant book of 1929 — certainly a transitional phase in his thought — Heidegger developed the idea of a finite metaphysics inasmuch as he appealed to the role of the transcendental imagination but without wanting to draw the resolute consequences of Fichte and the other "absolute Idealists."[27] Once again that became interesting to me. No doubt this underlying problem here had also been given its profile in the comprehensive synthesis of Hegelian thought. Absolute knowledge is inseparable from the entire course of the spirit through all its ways of being conditioned and all its manifestations. As a thinker, Hegel was well aware of his own conditionedness and limitedness and hence of the room for improving the "philosophic science" he elaborated, and the goal of world history, the freedom of all, is in truth held in suspense even today, for perhaps understandable reasons, in the remoteness of a "bad infinity." The same ultimately holds true of the unity of history and of the system of philosophy that sustains Hegel's theoretic and historical work as a presupposition. Hermeneutical philosophy's point of truth is to recall these things.

This is the sense in which one of my earlier formulations has to be understood: "Dialectic has to be retrieved in hermeneutics."[28] This statement may not be reversed, at least not if with Hegel one understands under dialectic the unfolded form of philosophic demonstration and not simply that speculative element, which of course bestows upon all the ultimate basic propositions of philosophy from the days of Heraclitus onward, their tension-filled character. In contrast, Plato's art of dialogue and the "dialectic" of tireless self-correction of all abstract onesid-edness that the Socratic dialogue reflects can provide certain hints as to how a philosophic figure of thought may be constructed that reunites the metaphysical question concerning the infinite and absolute with the ineradicable finitude of the questioner. Plato himself designated the network of relationships among the *logoi* as "dialectic"; and this pertains to the being itself, which exposes itself to thought. By this he simultaneously meant that being itself may never be apprehended in the un-restricted presence of some *unus intuitus* ("unitary intuition") or of an infinite monad in the sense of Leibniz; but, as with all human clarity and lucidity, it is clouded over by opaqueness, passing away, and forgetfulness. Diotima knew this when she compared the knowing proper to humans with the life of a species that has its ongoing being only in the relentless process of the reproduction of its individual instances.[29] Hermeneutics tries to establish this point inasmuch as it characterizes the con-text of tradition within which we exist as an ongoing reacquisi-tion that proceeds into infinity. It endeavors to make its own just how every vital and productive conversation with someone else knows how to mediate the other's horizon with one's own.

So even the debate opened up by W. Pannenberg about her-meneutics and universal history, in which he sought to bring to my attention the consistency of Hegel's philosophy of history, seems to me finally not to have a real point of conflict.[30] There is indeed no disputing that the Christian and non-Christian histories of salvation — and even histories of un-salvation (*Un-heilsgeschichten*) such as the Nietzschean one of the mounting European nihilism — are a legitimate need of a human reason explicitly conscious of its historical character. To this extent universal history indisputably is an aspect of the experience of our historical character. Just like all other history, however, universal history too always must be rewritten insofar as it does not possess its absolute datum as does *Heilsgeschichte*; and each projection of universal history has a validity that does not last much longer than the appearance of a flash momentarily cutting across the darkness of the future as well as of the past as it gets lost in the ensuing twilight. That is the proposition of hermeneutical philosophy that I dared to defend against Hegel.

I would surely be the last to deny the primordial communality that unites all the thought attempts of humanity, including that of our Western tradition. So I have sought to reacknowledge, against Heidegger, that beginning (*Anfang*) in Plato and Platonism and also in Hegel (and not only in Schelling), which Heidegger's destruction of metaphysics was calling into question. I also would not dispute that, say, in Dilthey's thought, and still more in Graf Yorck motifs of *Lebensphilosophie* are operative that lead beyond the historical positivism to which Dilthey's epistemological foundation of the *Geisteswissenschaften* surrendered all too much.[31] Dilthey's passage from psychology to hermeneutics actually carries well beyond the methodology of the *Geisteswissenschaften,* and so brings him with inner consistency into proximity with Hegel. Everything that his school and his influence understood under the notion of objective spirit bears witness to this heritage.

On the other hand one has to see that each initiative in thought on the part of one who thinks, even when they all in the end inquire about the same thing, has to be profiled against the one who happens to be the partner of his philosophic conversation, if it is to be capable of articulation at all. When Heidegger made the introductory statement to Hegel's "Logic of Essence," "The truth of being is the essence" (*Die Wahrheit des Seins ist das Wesen*), the theme of that thought-provoking seminar on the occasion of the Freiburg jubilee of the year 1964, the intended profile that guided him was fully clear to me. I believed (and still believe), however, that Heidegger could have written this sentence himself — of course, in his sense and in his language. Then he would probably mean, "The unconcealment of being occurs as the 'coming-to-presence'" (*Die Offenbarkeit des Seins geschiet als das an-Wesen*). I have tried to set this down in a letter to him. Nonetheless Heidegger, in his answer to me, pushed the self-profiling so far that he totally distorted Hegel's statement and rendered it as follows: *Certitudo objectivitatis reflectitur qua relucentia* ("The certitude of objectivity is reflected as a shining back") and he explained it this way: "The intent of the seminar was to show forth how for Hegel it comes to the quite alienating determination of reflection as 'essence' (*Wesen*). To *see* this it is necessary from the outset to think truth as certitude and 'Being' as objectivity, in the transcendentality of absolute knowledge."[32]

A similar example, perhaps, would be that not only in Aristotle's notion of being as *ti en einai* but also in Hegel's notion of *Wesen* that "has been" (*gewesen ist*), the temporal horizon of being resounds, as precisely Heidegger had shown. In like manner he saw in Aristotle just as he had in Hegel the representative of the vulgar notion of time as measured time, which in fact constituted the object of their thematic analyses of the problem of time. In this respect it was obvious that both knew about time in another sense as well. That struck me as a problem and so I dedicated to Heidegger on the occasion of his eightieth birthday a piece on empty and fulfilled time that referred to other time experiences within the history of metaphysics (in Platonism and in Schelling and Hegel).[33] He replied to me that the actual counternotion for fulfilled time was not empty time but measured time. That is how strongly he was held fast in the will to have a profile.

Similarly Heidegger insisted on understanding Hegel's reflection in itself, which was certainly differentiated expressly enough from "extrinsic reflection," as testimony for the orientation toward self-consciousness that dominated Hegel, and he thus left Hegel's step to objective spirit underemphasized.

Nevertheless it is true of his own undertaking of posing the question of being anew and of overcoming the secular answer of metaphysics as well as the language of metaphysics that this new element belongs inextricably with the old. "Overcoming" presupposes the status of metaphysics for Heidegger's own thought not as something that lies behind him but as a partner against which he could be profiled.[34] Metaphyscs is just as much a presupposition for the overcoming of metaphysics and for Heidegger's "step back" (Schritt zurück) as is the total "oblivion of being" (Seinsvergessenheit) of the technological thought of our time.

I surely do not need to add that in my own attempt in *Truth and Method* I have proceeded equally (and onesidedly) in a profiling manner: with Schleiermacher whose hermeneutics I separated all too much from his dialectics; with Dilthey whom I measured against the consequences drawn by Heidegger and Nietzsche; and to be sure with Hegel, to whom for this reason I have devoted further studies and whose challenge I try to pose to myself, in positive as well as in negative aspects, wherever I can.

Notes

1. Acts 5:9. Compare *Werke*, 13, 29. The quotation comes up only in Michelet's edition, not in the manuscripts in Hegel's own hand; and it is related in a critical fashion to a "perspective of the various philosophies" that Hegel finds unsatisfactory but precisely *sub specie aeternitatis.*

2. It was the merit of Erich Rothacker's *Einleitung in die Geisteswissenschaften* (1920) to have demonstrated the historical debt of the historical school in relation to Hegel.

3. The most influential critique of Hegel's dialectic was that of Adolf Trendelenberg, who in turn obviously affected Hermann Cohen. The most visible manifesto of the movement "Back to Kant" was the book by Otto Liebmann, *Kant und die Epigonen* (1865).

4. See my 1971 essay, "Das ontologische Problem des Wertes," *Kleine Schriften* 4:205–217.

5. See Wilhelm Dilthey, *Die Jugundgeschichte Hegels* (1904) and Dilthey, *Gesammelte Schriften,* vols. 7–8.

6. See my presentation in *Truth and Method,* 146–150.

7. On the notion of facticity, compare Heidegger, *Being and Time*, trans. J. Macquarrie and E. Robinson, pp. 82–83, 225–226, passim.

8. The particular emphasis Heidegger put upon this point is documented now in his Marburg lecture series, *Logik. Die Frage nach der Wahrheit* (1925–1926) in which Aristotle's *Metaphysics,* bk. 9, ch. 10, is treated in detail in nos. 13b, 14.

9. As is well known, Heidegger's new turning first entered the public sphere after World War II in virtue of his *Brief über den Humanismus* (1947); but it was already substantially implied in some of his lectures, especially those on *Der Ursprung des Kunstwerks.* Both "Letter on Humanism" and "The Origin of the Work of Art" are available in English translation in *Basic Writings,* ed. David F. Krell (London: Routledge, Kegan Paul, 1975).

10. On Heidegger's later avoidance of the concept of hermeneutics, see *Unterwegs zur Sprache,* pp. 98, 120ff. English translation: *On the Way to Language,* ed. Peter D. Hertz (New York: Harper & Row, 1974).

11. My first publication in this area was my contribution in the festschrift for Richard Hamann (1939).

12. This was clear even before *Truth and Method,* in my 1958 lectures in Louvain (Chaire Cardinal Mercier, 1957), which have been published under the title, *La connaissance historique* (1963); now in English translation: "The Problem of Historical Consciousness," *Graduate Faculty Philosophy Journal/New School for Social Research* 5 (1975):8–52.

13. See my Plato book of 1931, *Platos dialektische Ethik* (2d ed., 1966), and especially my essay, *"Logos und Ergon in Platos Lysis," Kleine Schriften* 3:50–63; now also in English translation: *"Logos* and *Ergon* in Plato's *Lysis,"* in Gadamer, *Dialogue and Dialectic: Eight Hermeneutical Studies on Plato* (New Haven: Yale University Press, 1980), 1–20.

14. Collingwood's *Autobiography* has been translated at my instigation by J.

Finkeldei and published with an introduction by me under the title, *Denken* (1955).

15. See my recent piece, "Hermeneutics as a Theoretical and Practical Task" as well as my contribution to the Congress in Thessaloniki (1978) on Aristotle's practical philosophy (in press).

16. On this rests the universality of hermeneutics, which furnishes the object of the discussion in the Suhrkamp volume, *Hermeneutik und Ideologierkritik* (Frankfurt 1971).

17. Hegel, "Vorrede," *Wissenschaft der Logik*.

18. See Aristotle, *Eth. Nic.* K7, 1177b$_{31}$ff.

19. Herbert Marcuse, *Hegels Ontologie und die Grundzüge einer Theorie der Geschichtlichkeit*, 1st ed. (Frankfurt, 1932).

20. Compare the concluding sentence in Heidegger's Habilitationsschrift, *Die Kategorien- und Bedeutungslehre von Duns Scotus* (1916). There he speaks of "the great task of a foundational confrontation with the system of a historical *Weltanschauung* that is the most forcible in fullness as well as in depth, experiential richness, and concept-formation, which sublated in itself all prior fundamental philosophic problem motifs, namely, with Hegel."

21. From a letter of Heidegger of 2 December 1971: "I myself do not know clearly enough how my 'position' vis-à-vis Hegel is to be determined — it would not be enough to put it down as a 'counterposition'; the determination of 'position' is connected with the question concerning the mystery of the 'beginning' (*Anfangs*); it is far more difficult, because simpler than the explanation Hegel gives for it before the start of the 'movement' in his *Logik*. — I have repeatedly opposed the talk about the 'breakdown' of the Hegelian system. What has broken down, that means to have sunk away, is what came after Hegel — Nietzsche included."

22. *Hegels Dialektik. Fünf hermeneutische Studien* (1971). The letters of Heidegger cited in the afterword are in reference to this publication. This work has been translated into English: *Hegel's Dialectic. Five Hermeneutical Studies* (New Haven: Yale University Press, 1976). The fourth essay from the German original has been omitted and replaced with the essay referred to in n.23.

23. "Hegels Dialektik des Selbstbewusstseins," *Materialien zu Hegels Phaenomenologie des Geistes* (Frankfurt: Suhrkamp 1973), pp. 217–242; English: "Hegel's Dialectic of Self-consciousness," 54–74.

24. Now published as "Heidegger und die Sprache der Metaphysik," in *Kleine Schriften* 3:212–220.

25. In the letter mentioned in n. 28, Heidegger himself made the following remark about my Freiburg lecture on "Hegel and Heidegger" (pp. 100–116): "But I think you bring the dialectic of consciousness and of 'being' too closely together with the Platonic dialectic — in view of the 'conversation' perhaps justifiably." This admission was precisely my concern and what I explicitated somewhat further in my memorial speech, "Sein Geist Gott," *Kleine Schriften* 4:74ff.

26. The widespread prejudice that Aristotle placed the ideal of the theoretic life first on account of his dependence upon Platonism while in fact, however, the practical-political ideal of life was the consequent outcome of the argument of the *Ethics,* I opposed in my lecture in Thessaloniki: "We are not placed before the choice whether we will be gods or human beings."

27. See "Kant und die philosophische Hermeneutik," *Kleine Schriften* 4:196–204.

28. From a letter of Heidegger of 29 February 1972: "Insofar as I have looked over your studies on Plato and Hegel and thought them through, they clarify and at the same time ground the suggestion with which you close your Freiburg lecture: 'Dialectic has to be retrieved in hermeneutics.' — Thereby is productively opened up for the first time a way towards getting over (*Verwindung*) dialectic. The closer specification of hermeneutics nevertheless at the same time forces us to the question whether and in which way the peculiarly universal claim of information-technique can be recovered in hermeneutics as a deficient (in the utmost measure) mode of 'mutual understanding' in hermeneutics. — The assumption of both tasks has for its execution not only to suffer through and acknowledge the linguistic poverty of thought, but to ponder it in a way that precedes all reflection and is on the way toward an initial 'de-termination' (*Be-Stimmung*) of phenomenology."
Heidegger is surely correct when he regards information technique as an extreme case that poses for hermeneutics its utmost task. But even here I ask what the linguistic poverty of speech really means. In his letter Heidegger continues: "Why does thinking necessarily remain in the language-poverty of word discovery? Presumably because the utterance of thinking has to utter being (even more so, its difference from entities), while any given historical language still addresses and expresses the entity in a way that is oblivious of itself. The word is fashioned for the uttering of entities. But it is again only capable of so speaking, because it speaks out of the lighting-up-process of being, and speaking even names this. Indeed how enigmatic are the names of *this* naming. How does it stand with the hermeneutics of *such names?*"
I would like to suggest that here for Heidegger because he so looks to names and naming and suggests speaking about the "enigmatic" metaphoricity. But does not a metaphor become enigmatic precisely by reason of the fact that it becomes dissociated as a name from the *ductus* of the discourse? Must not the poverty of language arise instead from the ideal of naming itself and get overcome as it were by itself in the dialogical movement of thought?

29. See Plato's *Symposium*, 207ff.

30. Wolfhart Pannenberg, "Hermeneutik und Universalgeschichte," *Zeitschrift für Theologie und Kirche* 60 (1963):90–121.

31. Collingwood especially has stressed and criticized this in his *Idea of History*. On the other hand, recent investigators try to stress the positivistic side in Dilthey with a positive intent. See the well-balanced presentation by Manfred Riedel, *Verstehen oder Erklären?* (1978), esp. 42ff.

32. The precise context of the passages cited from Heidegger's letter of 2 December 1971 is: "In order to go into the question as to whether on p. 94 you have 'noticed something correct,' I refer you to both the enclosed photos that Schadewalt sent me last September [Marginal comment: the thrice underlined *'en'* in *'to ti en einai'* the already *has been* of mediation.]

"The intention of the seminar was to demonstrate how for H. [Hegel] it comes to the quite alienating determination of reflection as 'essence' (*Wesen*).

"To see this it is necessary beforehand to think about the truth as certitude and 'being' as objectivity in the transcendentality of absolute knowledge.

"The sentence, 'The truth of Being is Essence' [*Die Wahrheit des Seins ist das Wesen*], in Latin would have to go: Certitudo objectivitatis +) reflectitur qua relucentia. But even in this way the Latin language does not speak philosophically in Hegel's sense as you convincingly demonstrate.

"If Oskar Becker were still alive — by the way, an outstanding picture from Schadewalt — he could testify that already in 1922 I spoke of the *Reluzenz* in *Dasein*. The word is meant to say something other than reflection as an act of consciousness — namely the shining back of the coming-to-presence [*des Anwesens*] upon and within *Dasein*. This belongs to the Descartes critique attempted in the first Marburg lecture.

"Accordingly, the working note of page 67 is to be thought about in a different way. 'The undomesticated element' (*Das Unheimische*) does not consist in the fact that reflection 'can settle down nowhere,' but in the fact that the 'aletheia' itself and as such is *not* experienced and grounded, that it does not come to 'Wesen' (verbally construed as 'presencing') as the *'Ereignis'* ('appropriation') cf. the lecture on Identity.

"This experiencing of 'aletheia' is the step back to the 'most ancient of what is ancient' (cf. *Aus der Erfahrung des Denkens*, p. 19), the turning to the 'other beginning,' i.e. the one and the same single beginning of Western European thought, but this beginning of thought in another manner. While for decades I already thought and tried to cherish this tradition, I fell into the completely inadequate talk about the '*Sprung*' ('leap') in a lecture, 'Der Satz der Identität,' that was contemporaneous with the Jubilee seminar under discussion; if you were to see my copy, you could verify the corrections I made immediately when I had the printed text in front of me. This briefly in response to your rhetorical questions, p. 90, section 2, below."

33. Now in *Kleine Schriften* 3:221–236.

34. Heidegger himself had thoroughly recognized this connection and set himself later against the misuse of his slogan about the "overcoming (*Ueberwindung*) of metaphysics." He suggested as a new expression "the getting over (*Verwindung*) of metaphysics"; and in my essay on "Hegel and Heidegger" I have explained this new turn of speech: What one gets over does not simply lie behind one as simply overcome or eliminated but keeps on determining one.

What Is Practice?
The Conditions of Social
Reason

Today practice tends to be defined by a kind of opposition to theory. There is an antidogmatic tone to the word *practice,* a suspicion against the merely theoretic, rote knowledge of something of which one has no experience whatsoever. To be sure this polarity has been constantly present; and antiquity was also familiar with it. But the opposed concept, the concept of theory, has become something different in our time and has lost its dignity. It suggests nothing of what *theoria* was to the eye disciplined enough to discern the visibly structured order of the heavens and the order of the world and of human society. Theory has become a notion instrumental to the investigation of truth and the garnering of new pieces of knowledge. That is the basic situation in terms of which our question, What is practice? is first motivated. But we are no longer aware of this because in starting from the modern notion of science when we talk about practice, we have been forced in the direction of thinking of the application of science.

If the public awareness thinks of practice in this fashion as the application of science, then what is science? What novel and singular turning by modern science has led to the transformation of practice into the anonymous and all but unaccounted for (on the part of science at least) application of science? Science is no longer the quintessence of knowledge and of what is worth knowing, but a way. It is a way of advancing and penetrating into unexplored and unmastered realms. Such a forward thrust and progress was not to be gained without a primary renunciation. The first creator of modern science, Galileo (the founder of classical mechanics), can illustrate this. But what cleverness it took for Galileo to work out the laws of free fall at a time when no one could have observed a free fall empirically, since it was only in post-Galileian times that a vacuum was experimentally produced. What the experiment that was so fascinating to us in school, in which the goose feather falls at the same rate of speed as the lead pellet in a vacuum, actually confirms, Galileo had already performed ahead of time by means of an enormous anticipation of the mind. This is the way Galileo himself described it: *mente concipio* — in my mind I apprehend the idea of the free fall, which, unobstructed by any medium, may be formulated in terms of its purely mathematical regularity with respect to the correlation of distance and time.

In this fashion science in principle takes on a new attitude. In prescinding from the primarily experienceable and familiar totality of our world, it has been developed into a knowledge of manipulable relationships by means of isolating experimentation. Hence its relation to practical application is to be understood as integral to its modern essence. If abstract relations between initial and terminal limiting conditions become graspable and calculable in such a way that the positing of new initial conditions has a predictable outcome, then the hour of technology has arrived by way of science as understood in this way. The old relationship of the products of the arts and crafts with the models furnished by nature has thus been transformed into an ideal of construction, into the ideal of a nature artificially produced in accord with an idea.

That is what has ultimately brought about the civilizational pattern of modernity in which we live. The ideal of construction implicit in the scientific concept of mechanics has become an arm prolonged to monstrous proportions. This has made possible the nature of our machines, our transformation of nature, and our outreach into space.

The immanent consequence of this nexus between methodical construction and technical production has had a double effect. First, technology, like the craftsmanship of old, is integrally related to a preconceived project. The average economy of the medieval world or of the other high civilizations of humanity always subordinated technical endeavor to the command of the users. The one who ultimately set the standard for what was to be made was the user. Obviously that was determinative for the ancient mode of labor. On the contrary, we can observe with our own eyes how in our civilization, characterized by technological growth, what has been artificially produced sets the new terms — as a consumer-awakening and need-stimulating industry is built up around us. Second, what necessarily becomes pervasive on account of this ever more artificial world is the loss of flexibility in our interchange with the world. Whoever makes use of technology — and who does not? — entrusts himself to its functioning. It is by means of a primary renunciation of freedom in relation to one's own overall ability to act that one has come into the enjoyment of these astonishing comforts and enlargements of wealth that modern technology makes available to us.

Two things have become obscure for us on account of this. For whose benefit is the work being accomplished? And how much do the achievements of technology serve life? From this there arises in a new way the problem that has been posed in every civilizational context, the problem of social reason.

The technologizing of nature and of the natural environment, with all its far-reaching effects, stands under the rubric of rationalization, demystification, demythologization, the dismantling of overhasty anthropomorphic correspondences. At last economic feasibility, the new balance wheel of the relentless process of change in our century, becomes an ever stronger social force. All this is characteristic of the maturity or, if you will, the crisis of our civilization, for the twentieth century is the first to be determined anew in a decisive fashion by technology, with the onset of the transfer of technical expertise from the mastery of the forces of nature to social life. This occurrence was somewhat belated. In the eighteenth century there were prophets of the new future of society, but the massive supporting forces of European and Western culture, Christianity, humanism, the heritage of antiquity, and the old forms of political organization remained determinative. With the French Revolution a new lower estate, the third estate, entered decisively into social life, and because it too lived for the most part as conditioned by religion, once again the unhindered and resolute application of technological capacities to social life was postponed.

But now we have already gone that far. Not that our society has been completely determined by the social technologists, but a novel expectation has become pervasive in our awareness: whether a more rationalized organization of society or, briefly, a mastery of society by reason and by more rational social relationships may not be brought about by intentional planning. This is the ideal of a technocratic society, in which one has recourse to the expert and looks to him for the discharging of the practical, political, and economic decisions one needs to make. Now the expert is an indispensable figure in the technical mastery of processes. He has replaced the old-time craftsman. But this expert is also supposed to substitute for practical and political experience. That is the expectation the society places on him and which he, in the light of a sober and methodical self-appraisal and an honest heightening of awareness, cannot fulfill.

Still more perilous is the effect of the technical penetration of society by means of the technologizing of the formation of public opinion. Today this is perhaps the strongest new factor in the play of social forces. The modern technology of information has made available possibilities that make necessary the selection of information to a heretofore unimaginable extent. Any selection, however, means acting in the name of everyone else; that cannot be otherwise. Whoever does the selecting withholds something. If he were not to make a selection, things would be still worse. Then one would lose the last remnant of understanding to the relentless stream of information by which one is flooded. It is inevitable, then, that the modern technology of communication leads to a more powerful manipulation of our minds. One can intentionally steer public opinion in certain directions and exercise influence on behalf of certain decisions. Possession of the news media is the decisive issue, which is why in every democracy more or less impotent attempts have been made in the administration and structuring of the public news media to bring about balance and control. That this is never accomplished to the degree that the consumer of the news can be assured of a genuine satisfaction of his need for information is clear from the increasing apathy of mass society with regard to public affairs.

The increase in the degree of information, then, does not necessarily mean a strengthening of social reason. Instead it seems to me that the real problem lies right here: the threatening loss of identity by people today. The individual in society who feels dependent and helpless in the face of its technically mediated life forms becomes incapable of establishing an identity. This has a profound social effect. Here lies the greatest danger under which our civilization stands: the elevation of adaptive qualities to privileged status.

In a technological civilization it is inevitable in the long run that the adaptive power of the individual is rewarded more than his creative power. Put in terms of a slogan, the society of experts is simultaneously a society of functionaries as well, for it is constitutive of the notion of the functionary that he be completely concentrated upon the administration of his function. In the scientific, technical, economic, monetary processes, and most especially in administration, politics, and similar forms, he has to maintain himself as what he is: one inserted for the sake of the smooth functioning of the apparatus. That is why he is in demand, and therein lie his chances for advancement. Even when the dialectic of this evolution is sensible to each one who asserts that ever fewer people are making the decisions and ever more are manning the apparatus, modern industrial society is oppressed by immanent structural pressures. But this leads to the degeneration of practice into technique and — through no fault of the experts themselves — to a general decline into social irrationality.

In this situation what significance can there be in philosophic reflection on the true meaning of practice? I start with a perhaps unexpected point, a point that, when everything is considered, seems to be the deepest because it constitutes the immutable anthropological background for all the human and social changes, past or present. What has occurred in nature when a being has emerged within the chain of the formations of nature or creation, a being which turned away from the interlocking of every living creature in its instinctual schemes and its relation to the preservation of the species?

Human being is an essence whose vital instinct has been so atrophied that in contrast to everything else with which we are familiar in the animal realm, it possesses an indisputable specificity. The latter is not diminished in the least by the study of animal societies and their forms of communication, solidarity, and aggression. This special human dimension is the in-built capacity of man to think beyond his own life in the world, to think about death. This is why the burial of the dead is perhaps the fundamental phenomenon of becoming human. Burial does not refer to a rapid hiding of the dead, a swift clearing away of the shocking impression made by one suddenly stuck fast in a leaden and lasting sleep. On the contrary, by a remarkable expenditure of human labor and sacrifice there is sought an abiding with the dead, indeed a holding fast of the dead among the living. We stand amazed before the wealth of mourning gifts that continually flows up toward us from the graves of every ancient culture. Gifts of mourning are a way of cherishing human existence. They do not let death have the last word. We have to regard this in its most elementary significance. It is not a religious affair or a transposition of religion into secular customs, mores, and so on. Rather it is a matter of the fundamental constitution of human being from which derives the specific sense of human practice; we are dealing here with a conduct of life that has spiraled out of the order of nature. As compelling as the vital instincts that we can observe are, say, among birds, how astonishing is their shunning of dead members of the species or their total indifference toward them. This contrast points up how humanity has begun to be turned against the natural vital instincts of survival.

From this starting point, we can learn the essential traits of specifically human practice. First there is labor. Hegel has quite rightly shown what an overwhelming achievement of renunciation work entails. It consists of obstructed desires: whoever works is not just out after the immediate satisfaction of needs. Consequently the product of labor never belongs to the individual alone. Especially when the world of labor is organized according to a division of labor, it belongs to the society. For society in its initial stages, the first thing formed is language. What is language? Where does language go beyond the silent agreement of the sort we observe among ants or bees? Aristotle noticed the decisive factor: a being that has language is characterized by a certain distance in relation to what is present at any given moment, for language brings about presence. By entertaining remote goals in the present, we make a choice of action in the sense of choosing means suited to given ends, and beyond this, we hold fast to the binding norms in the light of which human action is projected as something intrinsically social.

This involves a first step toward what we call practice. In the kind of being whose needs and goals have become complex and even contradictory, there is a need for enlightened choice, just deliberation, and right subordination under common ends. One thinks of the hunting societies of primitive history and the remarkable social achievements to which men even then had advanced. The greatest of these is the stabilization of norms of conduct in the sense of right and wrong. This arises out of the background of a fundamental instability of human nature unique in the realm of nature. Its most mysterious expression is the phenomenon of war, which has stirred the particular interest of contemporary ethnology and prehistory. It seems to be the strangest discovery of this twisted nature called man, and it appears to be a contradiction within nature itself to have produced a type of being that can turn against itself in such a way that in a planned and organized fashion it attacks, destroys, or maims fellow members of its own species.

We have to keep in full view the entire range of the human — from the cult of the dead and concern with what is just, to war — in order to apprehend the true meaning of human practice. It is not exhausted in collective and functional adaptation to the most natural conditions for life, as we can verify among animals that form a state. Human society is organized for the sake of a common order of living, so that each individual knows and acknowledges it as a common one (and even in its breakdowns, in crime). It is precisely the excess beyond what is necessary for the mere preservation of life that distinguishes his action as human action.

To be sure, we have also started to become gradually aware of how even for other products of nature, plants as well as animals, the rational teleological scheme of an economy of nature that does nothing in vain is too narrow. But where behavior involves consciously intended purposiveness, in terms of which one understands oneself as humanly reasonable, because one has an insight into the suitability of any means to commonly willed ends, the realm of all that transcends utility, usefulness, purposiveness takes on a unique distinction. We call anything of this sort beautiful in the same sense in which the Greeks used the word *kalon*. This referred not just to the creations of art or ritual, which are beyond the realm of necessities, but it encompasses everything with respect to which one understands without any question that because it is choiceworthy, it is neither capable nor in need of a justification of its desirability from the standpoint of its purposiveness. This is what the Greeks called *theoria*: to have been given away to something that in virtue of its overwhelming presence is accessible to all in common and that is distinguished in such a way that in contrast to all other goods it is not diminished by being shared and so is not an object of dispute like all other goods but actually gains through participation. In the end, this is the birth of the concept of reason: the more what is desirable is displayed for all in a way that is convincing to all, the more those involved discover themselves in this common reality; and to that extent human beings possess freedom in the positive sense, they have their true identity in that common reality.

But what kind of stories from olden times are these? How do the realities of today's world look? Where do we have such a transparency in the communal character of the ways of life in our society? And has there ever been such a thing? How was it in the days of the shocking circumstances of slavery? And in any case does there not grow up out of the necessity of a division of labor and out of the necessary differences in needs and in their satisfaction an inevitable shrinkage of such a communality, such as is displayed in quasi-natural relationships of leadership and service? Does not the nature of the reality itself dictate that this relationship be transformed into that of master and slave?

On the part of the most reflective among the critics of our society, this is formulated today as the suspicion of ideology. For all the putative communality of the ruling interests, is it not really a matter of interests in a domination that has been established by means of naked force and then been declared to be in the name of freedom and as a free constitution? Neo-Marxists call this distorted communication. Even language, which affords the most properly communal and communicative factor, is said to be deformed by the interests of oppressive domination. It is said to be an aim of emancipatory reflection, of completely achieved enlightenment, to eliminate this nonidentity. This means getting rid of the lack of self-understanding in what is communicated linguistically as the common world and regaining individual and social identity. Emancipatory reflection is supposed to achieve this by elevating the situation to a state of reflective consciousness, and to the degree that it does make things reflectively conscious, it eliminates what as divisive and obstructive has hindered the society's authentic flow of communication for the sake of what is common. That is the claim of the critique of ideology.

As a model for what it promises to achieve, the proponents of the critique of ideology always appeal to psychoanalysis, the psychoanalytic overcoming of such losses of identity. The claim of the critique of ideology is that one could also bring this about within the state and the society. By reflection, by the completion of enlightenment, and in a conversation free of coercion, the repressions and social deformations would be dismantled — with the aim, as, say, Habermas formulates it, of realizing communicative competence. By such competence one is enabled, beyond all distinctions, to communicate, to talk reciprocally, and to attain agreement by insight.

But of course the model of psychoanalysis aims at the reinsertion of the disturbed individual into an already existing, communicatively interconnected society. This is evident in that psychoanalysis presupposes the patient's insight that he or she is sick. A psychoanalytic treatment could never be successful if someone were to pursue this course with resistance and involuntarily and without any real sense of his genuine helplessness. The model is viable only to the degree that there, too, one is dealing with the reestablishment of distorted conditions within the community of communication.

In my eyes this has a negative and a positive side. First, the work of ideology critique has a dialectical structure. It is related to determinate social conditions upon which it has corrective and dismantling effects. It belongs itself, then, to the social process that it criticizes. That is the ineluctable presupposition that cannot be replaced by any scientific pretension. This is ultimately no less true for psychoanalysis. However often technical-scientific skill may intervene in psychoanalytic therapy, there is always a moment of authentic practice present as well. Nothing is "made" here or produced by construction, not even the life story of the patient. The constructive hypotheses of the therapist have to be accepted by the personal reflection of the patient. This goes far beyond any technical procedure inasmuch as it puts the patient in his entire social and mental constitution to free, spontaneous work on his own healing.

Utopia too contains an indirect relationship with the authentic notion of practice. Here it is utterly clear: utopia is a dialectical notion. Utopia is not the projection of aims for action. Rather the characteristic element of utopia is that it does not lead precisely to the moment of action, the "setting one's hand to a job here and now." A utopia is defined by the fact that (as I once had occasion to call it) it is a form of suggestiveness from afar. It is not primarily a project of action but a critique of the present. This may be gleaned from the Greeks. They have already shown what this means. What Plato brings before us in his *Republic* or his *Laws,* what we are familiar with from traces elsewhere as evidence of the whole literary genre of utopia among the Greeks, or that which we know of, is distinguished by the way it often mediates an insight into the present and its weaknesses by means of a portrait deformed even to the point of the grotesque. Think, for instance, about the role played by the community of wives and children in the Platonic *Republic.* It is a provocative invention in which Plato examines by means of a very clear statement the retrograde function of familial dynasties in the social life of the Greek polis. It seems terribly naive to me, when one tries to soften the utopian character of the Platonic writings as much as possible by saying something like the following: But at least something of what Plato portrays could still be realized. Everything he describes ought to be realized but not by means of the compulsory ordering Plato prescribed there.

The point is that genuine solidarity, authentic community, should be realized. The quintessence of Plato's knowledge was that only friendship with oneself makes possible friendship with others. It would be a long tale to tell about how Plato demonstrated this also in his practical political life as an adviser in that unhappy Sicilian adventure about which we are so well informed by his letters, especially the Seventh Letter. The Platonic utopia is only supposed to make a conceptual distinction intelligible:

the difference between wishing or desiring and choosing. Wishing is defined by the way it remains innocent of mediation with what is to be done. That is in truth what wishing is. This is not to say anything against wishing. I would even suggest that Ortega y Gasset was presumably right when he said, Technology will run aground on its lack of imagination, of the power to wish.

It is the creative capacity of human beings to come up with wishes and to try to find ways to satisfy them, but that does not change the fact that wishing is not willing; it is not practice. Practice consists of choosing, of deciding for something and against something else, and in doing this a practical reflection is effective, which is itself dialectical in the highest measure. When I will something, then a reflection intervenes by which I bring before my eyes by means of an analytical procedure what is attainable: If I will this, then I must have that; if I want to have this, then I have to have this . . . ; until at last I come back to my own situation, where I myself can take things in hand. To speak with Aristotle, the conclusion of the practical syllogism and of practical deliberation is the resolve. This resolve, however, together with the whole path of reflection, from the willing of the objective to the thing to be done, is simultaneously a concretization of the willed objective itself. For practical reason does not consist simply in the circumstance that one reflects upon the attainability of the end that he thinks good and then does what can be done. Aristotle distinguishes very explicitly the mere resourcefulness that for any given ends finds the right means with almost inhuman skillfulness (which means lying whenever necessary, deceiving wherever possible, talking one's way out of anything). This sharpness of the operator is no real "practical reason." With the latter the point, which is delimited against any technical rationality, is that the aim itself, the "universal," derives its determinacy by means of the singular. We are familiar with this in many areas of our social experience. We are familiar with it from the jurisprudence of all times. What the law prescribes, what a case of a given law is, is only determined unequivocally in the eyes of a formalist who endangers life. Finding the law means thinking the case together with the law so that what is actually just or the law gets concretized. For this reason the body of precedents (the decisions already laid down) is more crucial for the legal systems than the universal laws in accord with which the decisions are made. This is correct insofar as the meaning of any universal, of any norm, is only justified and determined in and through its concretization. Only in this way, too, is the practical meaning of utopia filled in. It, too, is not a guide for action but a guide for reflection.

All these are characteristic forms of "practice." One does not "act" inasmuch as one executes one's freely and well-thought-out plans, but practice has to do with others and codetermines the communal concerns by its doing.

Practice, then, certainly does not rely solely upon an abstract consciousness of norms. It is always concretely motivated already, prejudiced to be sure, but also challenged to a critique of prejudices. We are always dominated by conventions. In every culture a series of things is taken for granted and lies fully beyond the explicit consciousness of anyone, and even in the greatest dissolution of traditional forms, mores, and customs the degree to which things held in common still determine everyone is only more concealed. This is basically acknowledged by Hegel's doctrine of determinate negation. But to me it appears to be a quite important insight that has been covered over in our day by historicism and all the varieties of relativist theory. Perhaps one might ask, Is this perhaps already available remnant of things held in common (which constitutes the basis upon which state and society can exist at all) sufficient, so that, for example, a witness at a trial still tells the truth even though there is no religiously sanctioned oath that binds him? If this is all that one should again become expressly conscious of by means of a reflection concerning practice, is this not too little?

But maybe this is too negative a perspective. Perhaps the normative character of practice and hence the efficacy of practical reason is "in practice" still a lot greater than theory thinks it is. It certainly looks at first as if we are being overwhelmed in our economic and social system by a rationalization of all the relations of life that follows an immanent structural compulsion so that we are always making new inventions, and we are always increasing the range of our technical activity without being able to see our way out of this vicious circle. Farseeing people already consider this a fatal path down which humanity is heading. But there are other, common experiences in this society atomized by the pursuit of profits. In the light of these experiences everyone can become expressly aware of the limits of manipulative capacities. I recall, for example, the genetic shudder, the shock wave that went through the world, when the CIBA colloquium devoted to the discussion of the possibilities of genetic breeding entered the public arena. Was it a moral awareness — or what kind of shock was it that arose in reaction to the idea that a kind of superman could be genetically bred while this society would be transformed into a worker-bee existence for the sake of these drones? Let us take another phenomenon — brainwashing. I still remember how in the early thirties brainwashing trials under Stalin were greeted with a sort of horror at a distance. To explain how such a turning round of consciousness was carried out, one hit upon drugs or other types of manipulations.

Today we are utterly distraught by the premonition that the tendency toward conformity manifest in our world, as it is in every human society, might be the natural but hidden cause of the possibility of turning round long-enrooted convictions. In the face of such a manipulative capacity we turn away, here as well, not without a shudder. Or let us take a third instance: democracy. What kind of democracy is it that depends upon the photogenic qualities of the presidential candidates? Even if one readily concedes that no one becomes president only because of being photogenic but that it can be a condition without which he could not become president, do we not therefore ask ourselves with some concern how much this is a fulfillment of the practical-political meaning of democracy. Or let us take a final very mysterious problem of our technological world: the postponing of death. It presents an excessive demand upon a doctor of today that, counter to his Hippcratic oath, he "permits" someone to die. For a seemingly endless length of time he can carry on a meaningless, vegetative functioning of the organism with machine support. But sometime he has to summon the courage and, as I can tell you from many conversations with responsible doctors, take upon himself the torturous responsibility of saying, Now, an end to it!

Behind all these examples stands a more general experience, which as a whole appeals to our practical reason inasmuch as it makes us aware of the limits of our technical rationality: the ecological crisis. It consists of the fact that a potential outgrowth of our economy and technology on the path that we have hitherto been treading is leading in the foreseeable future toward making life on this planet impossible.

As all who are familiar with these matters will say to us, that is no more certain than that the calculated collision with one of the great celestial bodies would bring about the cosmic end of this planet. We owe this first supportive insight to science, and we owe much more to it as well. We are finally no longer living in the machine age with its huge extended arm, but we live in the age of cybernetics, of regulative systems, of self-steering systems. In virtue of the scientific enlightenment of our day we are starting to learn that there are equilibrium conditions and equilibrium states that need to be maintained. This insight is still provisionally restricted to very limited portions of our existence and has not yet risen to being a leading model of our experience of the world. But what announces its presence here is more than a technical problem.

The closed work place of the earth ultimately is the destiny of everyone. Maybe this awareness is slowly becoming pervasive by way of politics. One does not need to introduce anything new: Nixon surely had intrapolitical reasons for making the ecological crisis an issue of political conflict and would not have done so without such extraneous reasons. That does not take away from the fact that the cunning of history travels crooked paths. Nevertheless in this way the reality of the crisis has permeated the public awareness of peoples in industrialized countries.

I realize full well, what good can an industrialized country do, and especially one belonging to an economic bloc, without the cooperation of the other industrialized nations? And I have on numerous occasions experienced myself just how hopeless it is even to make clear to a less developed country the nightmare of an overdeveloped technology.

We are still a far cry from a common awareness that this is a matter of the destiny of everyone on this earth and that the chances of anyone's survival are as small as if a senseless attack with atomic weapons of destruction were to occur if humanity in the course of one or perhaps many, many crises, and in virtue of a history of experience involving many, many sufferings, does not learn to rediscover out of need a new solidarity. No one knows how much time we still have. But perhaps the principle is sound; for reason it is never too late. Then, too, one can never rely on the time calculations of the prophets of catastrophe. Such reckonings depend upon too many unknown variables to be able to expect reliable forecasts. And when one

becomes oppressed by occasionally far too pessimistic information, one can be consoled by remembering the period after the
invention of the railroad. Then psychiatrists, doctors, and so
forth predicted unanimously that this murderous racket of the
new means of transport would destroy mental health. If that
had been true, we would have all been crazy long ago. Maybe
we still have time even now.

Perhaps one finds this a rather sad consolation. But I do not
mean that this is all; it is but a beginning, an initial awareness
of solidarity. Merely out of necessity, to be sure. But is that a
real objection? Does it not rather say something for the availa-
bility of a *fundamentum in re*? Even a solidarity out of necessity
can uncover other solidarities.

Just as we, in our overstimulated process of progress of our
technological civilization, are blind to stable, unchanging elements of our social life together, so it could be with the reawak-
ening consciousness of solidarity of a humanity that slowly
begins to know itself as humanity, for this means knowing that
it belongs together for better or for worse and that it has to
solve the problem of its life on this planet. And for this reason
I believe in the rediscovery of solidarities that could enter into
the future society of humanity. I see certain traits of the Latin
world, which has adopted a protective posture opposed to the
profit making of the world with an astonishing power of resistance, a cheerfulness of natural living that we encounter in
southern countries as a sort of partial proof of a more stable
center of happiness and of the capacity to enjoy on the part of
human beings at large. I ask whether in foreign civilizations that
are now being drawn technologically over into the ambit of
European-American civilization — China, Japan, and especially
India — much of the religious and social traditions of their
ancient cultures does not still live on under the cover of European furnishings and American jobs, and whether whatever

lives on may not perhaps bring about an awareness out of necessity once again of new normative and common solidarities that let practical reason speak again.

Finally, I believe that bourgeois civilization still has a contribution to make. I do not mean this in the sense of the domination of one social class and its ideals of status. What can enter future world civilization through bourgeois civilization as the cultural inheritance of the West today may consist in more or less bourgeois or petty-bourgeois forms of enjoyment and of compensation for high-pressure reality. But the cunning of history travels crooked paths. It could be that what has been ingrained in us from a lengthy ancient and Christian history as an exemplar of humanity still lives on and can return to our reflective self-awareness, as we see today. And so, as a kind of answer to the question, What is practice? I would like to summarize: Practice is conducting oneself and acting in solidarity. Solidarity, however, is the decisive condition and basis of all social reason. There is a saying of Heraclitus, the "weeping" philosopher: The *logos* is common to all, but people behave as if each had a private reason. Does this have to remain this way?

Hermeneutics as Practical Philosophy

In itself hermeneutics is old. But in perhaps the last fifteen years it has taken on a new relevance. If we wish to assess this relevance and clarify the significance of hermeneutics and its relation to the central problems of philosophy and theology, we need to work out the historical background in the context of which the hermeneutical problem has taken on this fresh relevance. We have to trace the way hermeneutics has expanded from a specialized and occasional field of application to the vast field of philosophic questioning.

By hermeneutics is understood the theory or art of explication, of interpretation. The usual eighteenth-century German expression for this *Kunstlehre* (a teaching about a technical skill or know-how), is actually a translation of the Greek *techne*. It links hermeneutics with such *artes* as grammar, rhetoric, and dialectic. But the expression *Kunstlehre* points to a cultural and educational tradition other than that of late antiquity: the remote and no longer vital tradition of Aristotelian philosophy. Within it there was a so-called *philosophia practica* (*sive politica*), which lived on right up to the eighteenth century. It formed the systematic framework for all the "arts," inasmuch as they all stand at the service of the "polis."

To put ourselves right at the middle of the problematic, we have to submit the concepts involved in the nomenclature of the topic to a reflection upon their conceptual history. We might start with the word *philosophy* itself. In the eighteenth century it did not have the exclusive sense we attach to it when we distinguish philosophy from science, even while we still insist that it is a science as well — or even the queen of the sciences. At that time philosophy meant nothing other than science. By the same token, however, science did not consist simply of research grounded on the modern notion of method and deploying mathematics and measurement. It connoted both specialized knowledgeableness and any true knowledge, even if it were unattainable by means of the anonymous procedures of empirical scientific labor. Thus when Aristotle used the expression *practical philosophy,* by *philosophy* he meant "science" in that very general sense — indeed as knowledge using demonstration and generating doctrine, but not as the kind of science that for the Greeks was the model of theoretic knowledge (ἐπιστήμ): mathematics. This science is called political in contradistinction to theoretical philosophy as comprised by physics (knowledge of nature), mathematics, and theology (or first science, or metaphysics). Since the human being is a political being, political science belonged to practical philosophy as its most noble part, and it was cultivated under the title of classical politics right into the nineteenth century. In the light of this background the modern opposition between theory and practice seems rather odd, for the classical opposition ultimately was a contrast within knowledge, not an opposition between science and its application.

This implies at the same time that the original notion of practice (*praxis*) had quite a different structure too. In order to grasp it once again and to understand the meaning of the tradition of practical philosophy, one has to remove this notion completely from the context of opposition to science. It is not even the opposition to *theoria* (which is, of course, contained in the Aristotelian division of the sciences) that is really determinative here. This is manifest in the splended statement of Aristotle to the effect that we name active in the supreme measure those who are determined by their performance in the realm of thought alone. (*Pol.* 1325b 21ff.) *Theoria* itself is a practice (πρᾶξίς τις).

This strikes modern ears alone as a piece of sophistry because only for us is the significance of practice determined by the application of theory and science — with all the inherited connotations of practice which tend to connect with such application of theory every manner of impurity, haphazardness, accommodation, or compromise. In itself this is completely correct. Especially Plato constantly made this contrast more acute for us in his writings on the state. The ineradicable separation that exists between the purely ideal order and the soiled and mixed-up world of the senses (which dominates Plato's doctrine of the Idea) nevertheless is not identical with the relationship between theory and practice in the Greek sense. The conceptual range in which the word and concept *practice* have their proper place is not primarily defined by its opposition to theory as an application of theory. Especially as Joachim Ritter has shown in his works, practice formulates instead the mode of behavior of that which is living in the broadest sense. Practice, as the character of being alive, stands between activity and situatedness. As such it is not confined to human beings, who alone are active on the basis of free choice (*prohairesis*). Practice means instead the actuation of life (*energeia*) of anything alive, to which corresponds a life, a way of life, a life that is led in a certain way (*bios*). Animals too have *praxis* and *bios,* which means a way of life.

Of course there is a decisive difference between animal and human being. The way of life of human beings is not so fixed by nature as is that of other living beings. This is expressed by the concept of *prohairesis,* which can be predicated only of human being. *Prohairesis* means "preference" and "prior choice." Knowingly preferring one thing to another and consciously choosing among possible alternatives is the unique and specific characteristic of human being. The Aristotelian concept of practice has yet another specific emphasis inasmuch as it is applied to the status of a free citizen in the *polis.* This is where human practice exists in the eminent sense of the word. It is specified by the *prohairesis* of the *bios.* The free decision takes its bearings by the order of preferences guiding one's life conduct, whether it be pleasure, or power and honor, or knowledge. Besides these we encounter in the political makeup of human life together other differences in life conduct such as those between husband and wife, the elderly and the child, dependents and those who are independent (in former times chiefly the distinction between slave and free). All of this is "practice." So practice is here no longer the sheerly natural component within a mode of behavior, as is the case with animals set in the schemes of innate vital instincts. The sophistic enlightenment especially insisted that the whole *arete* (performative excellence) of human beings is utterly diverse in each case, even though the whole *arete* that rests upon knowing and choosing is only realized fully in the free status of the citizen of the polis.

Since "practice" comprises this broad range of significance, the most important delimitation that the concept of practice undergoes with Aristotle is not vis-à-vis theoretical science, which itself emerges from the enormous range of life possibilities as a type of the most noble practice. Rather it is the delimitation over against production based on knowledge, the *poiesis* that provides the economic basis for the life of the polis. In particular, if it is not a matter of the "lower servile" arts but of the kind a free man can engage in without disqualification, such a knowing and know-how pertain to his practice without being practical knowledge in the practical-political sense. And so practical philosophy is determined by the line drawn between the practical knowledge of the person who chooses freely and the acquired skill of the expert that Aristotle names *techne*. Practical philosophy, then, has to do not with the learnable crafts and skills, however essential this dimension of human ability too is for the communal life of humanity. Rather it has to do with what is each individual's due as a citizen and what constitutes his *arete* or excellence. Hence practical philosophy needs to raise to the level of reflective awareness the distinctively human trait of having *prohairesis,* whether it be in the form of developing those fundamental human orientations for such preferring that have the character of *arete* or in the form of the prudence in deliberating and taking counsel that guides action. In any case, it has to be accountable with its knowledge for the viewpoint in terms of which one thing is to be preferred to another: the relationship to the good. But the knowledge that gives direction to action is essentially called for by concrete situations in which we are to choose the thing to be done; and no learned and mastered technique can spare us the task of deliberation and decision. As a result, the practical science directed toward this practical knowledge is neither theoretical science in the style of mathematics nor expert know-how in the sense of a knowledgeable mastery of operational procedures (*poiesis*) but a unique sort of science. It must arise from practice itself and, with all the typical generalizations that it brings to explicit consciousness, be related back to practice. In fact, that constitutes the specific character of Aristotelian ethics and politics.

Not only is its object the constantly changing situations and modes of conduct that can be elevated to knowledge only in respect to their regularity and averageness. Conversely such teachable knowledge of typical structures has the character of real knowledge only by reason of the fact that (as is always the case with technique or know-how) it is repeatedly transposed into the concrete situation. Practical philosophy, then, certainly is "science": a knowledge of the universal that as such is teachable. But it is still a science that needs certain conditions to be fulfilled. It demands of the one learning it the same indissoluble relationship to practice it does of the one teaching it. To this extent, it does have a certain proximity to the expert knowledge proper to technique, but what separates it fundamentally from technical expertise is that it expressly asks the question of the good too — for example, about the best way of life or about the best constitution of the state. It does not merely master an ability, like technical expertise, whose task is set by an outside authority: by the purpose to be served by what is being produced.

All this holds true for hermeneutics as well. As the theory of interpretation or explication, it is not just a theory. From the most ancient times right down to our days, hermeneutics quite clearly has claimed that its reflection upon the possibilities, rules, and means of interpretation is immediately useful and advantageous for the practice of interpretation — whereas perhaps a fully worked out theory of logic has a more scientifically rarefied ambition than promoting the advance of logical thinking; just as number theory has a loftier aim than advancing calculative finesse. Hence, in a first approximation, hermeneutics may be understood as a teaching about a technical skill (*Kunstlehre*) in the manner of rhetoric too. Like rhetoric, hermeneutics can designate a natural capacity of human beings, and then it refers to the human capacity for intelligent interchange with one's fellows. So in a letter to his friend Hitzig, Johann Peter Hebel could say about a theologian that he "possesses and makes use of the most admirable of hermeneutics to understand and humanely interpret human foibles."

Thus the earlier hermeneutics was primarily a practical component in the activity of understanding and interpreting. It was far less frequently a theoretical textbook — which is practically what *techne* meant in antiquity — than a practical manual. Books bearing the title "Hermeneutics" usually had a purely pragmatic and occasional bent and were helpful for the understanding of difficult texts by explaining hard-to-understand passages. However, precisely in fields in which difficult texts have to be understood and interpreted, reflection upon the nature of such activity first evolved, and with this development something like hermeneutics in our contemporary sense was brought forth. This happened especially in the field of theology.

There we can find what is most important and most fundamental, for example, in Augustine's *De doctrina christiana*. Especially when he sought to become more precise about his stance toward the Old Testament, Augustine saw himself forced into a reflection that involved the meaning of "understanding" and compelled him to be clearer about the dogmatic claims of his texts. It was a theological task to discuss why the entire Old Testament cannot be an immediate mirror image or typological prefiguration of the Christian message of salvation. Things as contrary to Christian moral teaching as, say, the polygamy of the patriarchs could no longer be salvaged by allegorical interpretation and they made necessary a straightforward historical interpretation that drew upon knowledge of the remote and strange morality of the nomads, an essential differentiation of the scope of interpretation. As the Old Testament had been for earlier Christianity, so in the age of the Reformation the Holy Scriptures in their entirety became the object of a new hermeneutical preoccupation and the occasion of hermeneutical reflection. The allegorizing method of dogmatic interpretation of Scripture that prevailed in the Roman tradition and so permitted a dogmatic theological tradition to control the meaning of the Scripture was supposed to be overcome altogether in favor of the "Word of God." The new slogan of *sola scriptura* proved to be just as difficult a principle of interpretation. As much as it struggled against the dogmatic character of the Catholic tradition of interpretation, even Protestant exegesis was compelled to erect a certain dogmatic canon, and this meant that it had to reflect on the dogmatic results generated by the new reading of the Holy Scriptures in their original tongues. So it is that the new first principle, *sacra scriptura sui ipsius interpres,* became the source of a new theological hermeneutics. But what grew from this was not simply a doctrine concerning a technical skill (*Kunstlehre*); rather it also comprised a doctrine of the faith (*Glaubenslehre*).

Jurisprudence was another field in which reflection upon the interpretation of texts resulted not only from difficulties within hermeneutical practice but also from the material significance of these texts. In jurisprudence this reflection was mainly concerned with practical juridical questions that arose from the interpretation of legal texts and from their application in cases of conflict. Mediating the universality of the law with the concrete material of the case before the court is an integral moment of all legal art and science. These difficulties become particularly heightened wherever the legal texts are no longer the authentic expression of our experience of the law, rooted in our actual life experience, and represent instead a historical inheritance taken over from a completely different social and historical situation. A legal order that has become obsolete and antiquated is a constant source of legal difficulties, for meaningful interpretation requires adaptation to the actual situation. This general hermeneutical moment of all finding of law becomes even more pronounced in cases in which we speak of reception, particularly in the reception of Roman law in later Europe. However one might wish to evaluate this process of reception and however much a demythologizing of Romantic prejudices may be in order here, the process of making legal administration scientific was introduced with the assimilation of Roman-Italian legal skill north of the Alps. Under the historical conditions peculiar to the modern age, this process led also to the practice of hermeneutics and a theoretical heightening of awareness in the field of law. Thus the exempt status of the Caesar (*lege solutus*) under the Justinian code was a matter of dispute for years, and under the changed circumstances of modernity it became an ongoing hermeneutical thorn. The ideal of law implies the idea of equality under the law. If the sovereign himself is not subject to the law but can decide upon its application, the foundation of all hermeneutics is destroyed. Even this example demonstrates that the just interpretation of the law is not simply a doctrine concerning a technical skill (a type of logical subsumption under such and such a paragraph) but a practical concretization of the idea of the law. The art of the jurist is at the same time the administration of the law.

Another significant tension emerged from a very different direction, the resolution of which called for hermeneutics. With the rise of the new humanism, the great Latin and Greek classics, the models of all higher human culture, had to be appropriated anew. The return to classical Latin, as a somewhat exacting and fastidious novelty, particularly in view of its more refined style in comparison with the Latin of the scholastics, and especially the return to the Greek (and in the case of the Old Testament, to Hebrew) revealed the need for more than all sorts of hermeneutical aids regarding grammar, lexicons, and historical and factual information. This was supplied by the numerous resource manuals called "Hermeneutica." Beyond this chiefly informational aspect, the classics claimed a specific exemplary character that called into question the taken-for-granted self-awareness of modernity. By the same token, the famous *querelle des anciens et des modernes* belongs to the prehistory of hermeneutics insofar as it awakened a hermeneutical reflection upon the ideals of humanism. If this *querelle* has been correctly judged a preparation for the awakening of historical consciousness, then conversely this means that hermeneutics does not just inculcate facility in understanding; it is not a mere teaching concerning a technical skill. Rather it has to be able to give an account of the exemplary character of that which it understands.

As much as this contradicts the self-understanding of hermeneutics as a *Kunstlehre* — as is manifest in all its different facets — it is more than a mere teaching of a technique, and it belongs in the neighborhood of practical philosophy. And so it shares in the reference to self that is essential to practical philosophy. If, for example, ethics is a teaching about the right way to live, it still presupposes its concretization within a living ethos. Even the art of understanding the tradition, whether it deals with sacred books, legal texts, or exemplary masterworks, not only presupposes the recognition of these works but goes on further to shape their productive transmission. As long as it remained confined to normative texts, the earlier hermeneutics did not pose a central issue for the conception of problems of traditional philosophy. To that degree it is quite a long way from our contemporary interest in hermeneutics. Nevertheless, when the remoteness of the lofty and the remoteness of the recondite needed to be overcome not simply in specialized domains such as religious documents, texts of the law, or the classics in their foreign languages, but when the historical tradition in its entirety up to the present moment moved into a position of similar remoteness, the problem of hermeneutics entered intrinsically into the philosophic awareness of problems. This took place in virtue of the great breach in tradition brought about by the French Revolution and as a result of which European civilization splintered into national cultures.

With the disappearance of its validity as a thing to be taken for granted, the common tradition of the Christian states of Europe, which of course lived on, began to enter explicit consciousness in a completely novel way as a freely chosen model, as the passionate aim of nostalgia, and finally as an object of historical knowledge. This was the hour of a universal hermeneutics through which the universe of the historical world was to be deciphered. The past as such had become alien.

Every renewed encounter with an older tradition now is no longer a simple matter of appropriation that un-self-consciously adds what is proper to itself even as it assimilates what is old, but it has to cross the abyss of historical consciousness. The standard slogan became to return to the original sources, and in this fashion our historically mediated image of the past was placed on an entirely new footing. This involved a profoundly hermeneutical task. As soon as one acknowledges that one's own perspective is utterly different from the viewpoints of the authors and the meanings of the texts of the past, there arises the need for a unique effort to avoid misunderstanding the meaning of old texts and yet to comprehend them in their persuasive force. The description of the inner structure and coherence of a given text and the mere repetition of what the author says is not yet real understanding. One has to bring his speaking back to life again, and for this one has to become familiar with the realities about which the text speaks. To be sure, one has to master the grammatical rules, the stylistic devices, the art of composition upon which the text is based, if one wishes to understand what the author wanted to say in his text; but the main issue in all understanding concerns the meaningful relationship that exists between the statements of the text and our understanding of the reality under discussion.

The post-Romantic epoch did not actually do justice to this main issue in its development of hermeneutical procedures.

What happened was that the self-understanding that grew out of the tradition of teaching a technical skill (*Kunstlehre*) first presented itself to the experience of estrangement that emerged with historical consciousness, and so hermeneutics was conceived by the Romantics as a critical ability in dealing with texts. The mounting logical self-awareness of the inductive sciences came to the support of this self-understanding as a powerful aid. Accordingly one tried to follow the great model of the natural sciences and considered the ideal in both cases to be the exclusion of every subjective presupposition. Just as in natural scientific research the experiment that could be repeated by anyone affords the basis of verification, so too in the interpretation of texts one sought to apply procedures that anyone could check. The age-old procedures of exegesis, especially the gathering of parallels, underwent a historical-critical refinement at this time. On this basis the hermeneutic methodology that the Romantic interest subsumed under its scientific auspices was constantly compared with the methodology of the natural sciences. Its objects, the transmitted texts, were to be treated like the observational data in the scientific investigation of nature. This sort of self-understanding of the new critical philology also happens to correspond with Schleiermacher's separation of general hermeneutics from dialectics and, in the realm of theology, with his separation of the teaching of the technical skill of hermeneutics from the teaching of the faith (*Glaubenslehre*). That it was unable to do justice to the interest in history did not remain unnoticed by the great historians like Ranke or Droysen, for it did not match up to the theological pathos so alive in their critical research. Not without reason, they attached themselves to Fichte, Humboldt, and Hegel. In spite of this, there was no fundamental recognition of the older tradition of practical philosophy, even by Dilthey, who managed to articulate conceptually the heritage of the Romantic school. Insight into the connection between hermeneutics and practical philosophy was completely lacking.

Only when our entire culture for the first time saw itself threatened by radical doubt and critique did hermeneutics become a matter of universal significance. This had to it a persuasive inner logic. One has only to think of the radicalism in doubting that is to be found especially in Friedrich Nietzsche. His slowly growing influence in every area of our culture possessed a depth that is usually not sufficiently realized. Psychoanalysis, for instance, is scarcely imaginable without Nietzsche's radical calling into doubt of the testimony of human reflective self-consciousness. Nietzsche set the demand that one doubt more profoundly and fundamentally than Descartes, who had considered the ultimate unshakable foundation of all certitude to be explicit self-consciousness. The illusions of reflective self-consciousness, the idols of self-knowledge, constituted the novel discovery of Nietzsche, and later modernity may be dated in terms of the all-pervasive influence of Nietzsche. As a result, the notion of interpretation attained a far more profound and general meaning.

Now interpretation refers not only to the explication of the actual intention of a difficult text. Interpretation becomes an expression for getting behind the surface phenomena and data. The so-called critique of ideology called scientific neutrality into doubt. It questioned not merely the validity of the phenomena of consciousness and of self-consciousness (which was the case with psychoanalysis) but also the purely theoretical validity of scientific objectivity to which the sciences laid claim. The clear claim of Marxism was to the effect that the theoretical teachings of the sciences reflect with an intrinsic necessity the interests of the dominant social class, especially that of the entrepreneurs and capitalists. And one of the demands of Marxism, especially when trying to understand the manifestations of economic and social life, was to get behind the self-interpretations of bourgeois culture, which invoke the objectivity of science. In other ways too the philosophic career of the concept of interpretation, which has had such success in the last hundred years, has its philosophic grounding in the well-justified mistrust of the traditional framework whose basic terms are not so obvious and presuppositionless as they pretend to be. The preunderstanding implied in them lends an antecedent shape to the problems of philosophy in a definite way. But it not only schematizes philosophic thought; our entire cultural life bears witness to the oldest ontological provenance of our thought from Greek philosophy.

Heidegger's great merit was to have broken through the aura of obviousness with which the Greek thinkers used the concept of being. In particular, he laid bare the way modern thought was shaped by the completely unexplicated concept of consciousness that provides the principle of recent philosophy under the domination of the concept of being. His famous lecture, *What Is Metaphysics?* argued that traditional metaphysics did not ask the question of being itself (*die Frage nach dem Sein*) but on the contrary kept this question concealed, inasmuch as it constructed the edifice of metaphysics from the concept of being as the circumscribed already-out-there-now. The real intention of what was asked by Heidegger's question about being can be understood only in the light of the new concept of interpretation under discussion here. This becomes more evident when one weighs the title of the lecture word for word and catches the secret emphasis borne by the word *is*.

The intention of the question, What is metaphysics? is to inquire what metaphysics really is in contrast with what metaphysics wants to be and with what it understands itself to be. What was the significance of the fact that the question of philosophy took the shape of metaphysics? What is the significance of the event in which the Greek thinkers raised up their heads and freed themselves from the bonds of mythic and religious living and dared to put questions like, Why is it? and, What is it? and, Out of what does anything emerge into being? If one understands the question, What is metaphysics? in the sense that one asks what happened with the beginning of metaphysical thinking, then the Heideggerian question first acquires the force of its provocativeness and is disclosed as an instance of the new notion of interpretation.

The new notion of interpretation and consequently of hermeneutics that now enters the picture evidently surpasses the limits of any hermeneutic theory, no matter how universally understood. Ultimately it implies a totally new concept of understanding and self-understanding. Interestingly enough, the expression *self-understanding* today has become quite fashionable. It is constantly used even in current political and social discussions, not to mention popular fiction. Words are slogans. They often express what is missing and what should be. A self-understanding become unsure of itself is talked about by everyone. But it is the first appearance of a word that marks its succeeding history. The expression *self-understanding* was first used with a certain terminological emphasis by Johann Gottlieb Fichte. Because he felt he was dependent upon Kant, he claimed that his *Wissenschaftslehre* at the same time provided the single reasonable and authentic interpretation of Kantian philosophy. One ought to require coherence of a thinker. Only in the radical consistency of his thoughts would a philosopher be capable of attaining a genuine self-understanding. In Fichte's eyes, however, there is only one possible way to be completely and without contradiction in agreement with one's own thought, and that is when one derives everything that could claim validity in our thought from the spontaneity of self-consciousness and grounds it therein. If one were to affirm that besides his teaching on self-consciousness and the deduction of the root concepts, the categories, Kant assumed a thing-in-itself, and thus that mind is affected by the sense faculties, then one would have to affirm that he was not a thinker at all but a half-wit, as Fichte so shrilly and coarsely put it. Fichte took for granted that everything that is supposed to hold true must be brought forth by activity. By this he of course means a mental construction. And this has nothing to do with the absurd notion of solipsism that haunted the foothills of nineteenth-century philosophy. Construction, production, generation are transcendental concepts describing the inner spontaneity of self-consciousness and its self-unfolding. Only in this way may there be a real self-understanding on the part of thought.

Today this concept of self-understanding has broken down. Was it not a truly hybrid ambition to assert with Fichte and Hegel that the total sum of our knowledge of the world, of our "science," could be achieved in a perfect self-understanding? The famous title of Fichte's foundational philosophic work is indicative of this pretension. *"Wissenschaftslehre"* has nothing whatsoever to do with what is called 'philosophy of science' today. *"Wissenschaftslehre"* meant instead the all-encompassing knowledge consisting of the derivation of all the contents of the world from self-consciousness. It is characteristic of the new basic stance of philosophy and of the new insight brought home to us by the experiences of the last hundred years not only that this sense of science is no longer capable of being fulfilled but also that the meaning of self-understanding has to be understood differently.

Self-understanding can no longer be integrally related to a complete self-transparency in the sense of a full presence of ourselves to ourselves. Self-understanding is always on-the-way; it is on a path whose completion is a clear impossibility. If there is an entire dimension of unilluminated unconscious; if all our actions, wishes, drives, decisions, and modes of conduct (and so the totality of our human social existence) are based on the obscure and veiled dimension of the conations of our animality; if all our conscious representations can be masks, pretexts, under which our vital energy or our social interests pursue their own goals in an unconscious way; if all the insights we have, as obvious and evident as they may be, are threatened by such doubt; then self-understanding cannot designate any patent self-transparency of our human existence. We have to repudiate the illusion of completely illuminating the darkness of our motivations and tendencies. This is not to say, however, that we can simply ignore this new area of human experiences that looms in the unconscious. What comes in for methodical investigation here is indeed not only the field of the unconscious that concerns the psychoanalyst as a physician; it is just as much the world of the dominant social prejudices that Marxism claims to elucidate. Psychoanalysis and critique of ideology are forms of enlightenment, and both invoke the emancipatory mandate of the Enlightenment as formulated by Kant in terms of the "exodus from the condition of self-inflicted immaturity."

Nevertheless when we examine the range of these new insights, it seems to me that we need to cast a critical eye upon just what sort of untested presuppositions of a traditional kind are still at work in them. One has to ask oneself whether the dynamic law of human life can be conceived adequately in terms of progress, of a continual advance from the unknown into the known, and whether the course of human culture is actually a linear progression from mythology to enlightenment. One should entertain a completely different notion: whether the movement of human existence does not issue in a relentless inner tension between illumination and concealment. Might it not be just a prejudice of modern times that the notion of progress that is in fact constitutive for the spirit of scientific research should be transferable to the whole of human living and human culture? One has to ask whether progress, as it is at home in the special field of scientific research, is at all consonant with the conditions of human existence in general. Is the notion of an ever-mounting and self-perfecting enlightenment finally ambiguous?

If one wishes to appraise the significance or the task and the limits of what we call hermeneutics today, one must bear in mind this philosophic and humane background, this fundamental doubt about the legitimacy of objective self-consciousness. In a certain way, the very word *hermeneutics* and its cognate word *interpretation* furnish a hint, for these words imply a sharp distinction between the claim of being able to explain a fact completely through deriving all its conditions; through calculating it from the givenness of all its conditions; and through learning to produce it by artificial arrangement — the well-known ideal of natural scientific knowledge; and on the other hand, the claim (say, of interpretation), which we always presume to be no more than an approximation: only an attempt, plausible and fruitful, but clearly never definitive.

The very idea of a definitive interpretation seems to be intrinsically contradictory. Interpretation is always on the way. If, then, the word *interpretation* points to the finitude of human being and the finitude of human knowing, then the experience of interpretation implies something that was not implied by the earlier self-understanding when hermeneutics was coordinated with special fields and applied as a technique for overcoming difficulties in troublesome texts. Then hermeneutics could be understood as a teaching about a technical skill — but no longer.

Once we presuppose that there is no such thing as a fully transparent text or a completely exhaustive interest in the explaining and construing of texts, then all perspectives relative to the art and theory of interpretation are shifted. Then it becomes more important to trace the interests guiding us with respect to a given subject matter than simply to interpret the evident content of a statement. One of the more fertile insights of modern hermeneutics is that every statement has to be seen as a response to a question and that the only way to understand a statement is to get hold of the question to which the statement is an answer. This prior question has its own direction of meaning and is by no means to be gotten hold of through a network of background motivations but rather in reaching out to the broader contexts of meaning encompassed by the question and deposited in the statement.

What has to be held up as a first determination that will do justice to modern hermeneutics in contrast to the traditional kind is this notion that a philosophical hermeneutics is more interested in the questions than the answers — or better, that it interprets statements as answers to questions that it is its role to understand. That is not all. Where does our effort to understand begin? Why are we interested in understanding a text or some experience of the world, including our doubts about patent self-interpretations? Do we have a free choice about these things? Is it at all true that we follow our own free decision whenever we try to investigate or interpret certain things? Free decision? A neutral, completely objective concern? At least the theologian would surely have objections here and say, "Oh no! Our understanding of the Holy Scripture does not come from our own free choice. It takes an act of grace. And the Bible is not a totality of sentences offered willy-nilly as a sacrifice to human analysis. No, the gospel is directed to me in a personal way. It claims to contain neither an objective statement nor a totality of objective statements but a special address to me." I believe that not only theologians would have doubts about this notion that one ultimately encounters free decisions when interpreting transmitted texts. Rather there are always both conscious and unconscious interests at play determining us; it will always be the case that we have to ask ourselves why a text stirs our interest. The answer will never be that it communicates some neutral fact to us. On the contrary, we have to get behind such putative facts in order to awaken our interest in them or to make ourselves expressly aware of such interests. We encounter facts in statements. All statements are answers. But that is not all. The question to which each statement is an answer is itself motivated in turn, and so in a certain sense every question is itself an answer again. It responds to a challenge. Without an inner tension between our anticipations of meaning and the all-pervasive opinions and without a critical interest in the generally prevailing opinions, there would be no questions at all.

This first step of hermeneutic endeavor, especially the requirement of going back to the motivating questions when understanding statements, is not a particularly artificial procedure. On the contrary, it is our normal practice. If we have to answer a question and we cannot understand the question correctly (but we do know what the other wants to know), then we obviously have to understand better the sense of the question. And so we ask in return why someone would ask us that. Only when I have first understood the motivating meaning of the question can I even begin to look for an answer. It is not artificial in the least to reflect upon the presuppositions implicit in our questions. On the contrary, it is artificial not to reflect upon these presuppositions. It is quite artificial to imagine that statements fall down from heaven and that they can be subjected to analytic labor without once bringing into consideration why they were stated and in what way they are responses to something. That is the first, basic, and infinitely far-reaching demand called for in any hermeneutical undertaking. Not only in philosophy or theology but in any research project, it is required that one elaborate an awareness of the hermeneutic situation. That has to be our initial aim when we approach what the question is. To state this in words expressing one of our more trivial experiences, we must understand what is behind a question. Making ourselves aware of hidden presuppositions, however, means not only and primarily illuminating our unconscious presuppositions in the sense of psychoanalysis; it means becoming aware of the vague presuppositions and implications involved in a question that comes up.

The elaboration of the hermeneutic situation, which is the key to methodical interpretation, has a unique element to it. The first guiding insight is to admit of the endlessness of this task. To imagine that one might ever attain full illumination as to his motives or his interests in questions is to imagine something impossible. In spite of this, it remains a legitimate task to clarify what lies at the basis of our interests as far as possible. Only then are we in a position to understand the statements with which we are concerned, precisely insofar as we recognize our own questions in them.

In this connection, we must realize that the unconscious and the implicit do not simply make up the polar opposite of our conscious human existence. The task of understanding is not merely that of clarifying the deepest unconscious grounds motivating our interest but above all that of understanding and explicating them in the direction and limits indicated by our hermeneutic interest. In the rare cases in which the communicative intersubjectivity of the "community of conversation" is fundamentally disrupted so that one despairs of any intended and common meaning, this can motivate a direction of interest for which the psychoanalyst is competent.

But this is a limit situation for hermeneutics. One can sharpen any hermeneutic situation to this limit of despairing of meaning and of needing to get behind the manifest meaning. The labor of psychoanalysis would, it appears to me, be based on a false estimation of its legitimacy and its unique meaning, if its task were not regarded as a task at the limit and if it were not to set out from the fundamental insight that life always discovers some kind of equilibrium and that there also pertains to this equilibrium a balance between our unconscious drives and our conscious human motivations and decisions. To be sure, there is never a complete concord between the tendencies of our unconscious and our conscious motivations. But as a rule neither is it always a matter of complete concealment and distortion. It is a sign of sickness when one has so dissimulated oneself to oneself that one can know nothing further without confiding in a doctor. Then in a common labor of analysis, one takes a couple of steps further toward clarifying the background of one's own unconscious — with the goal of regaining what one had lost: the equilibrium between one's own nature and the awareness and language shared by all of us.

In contrast to this, the unconscious, in the sense of what is implicit to our direct awareness, is the normal object of our hermeneutic concern. This means, however, that the task of understanding is restricted. It is restricted by the resistance offered by statements or texts and brought to an end by the regaining of a shared possession of meaning, just as happens in a conversation when we try to shed light upon a difference of opinion or a misunderstanding.

In this most authentic realm of hermeneutic experience, the conditions of which a hermeneutic philosophy tries to give an account, the neighborly affinity of hermeneutics with practical philosophy is confirmed. First of all, understanding, like action, always remains a risk and never leaves room for the simple application of a general knowledge of rules to the statements or texts to be understood. Furthermore, where it is successful, understanding means a growth in inner awareness, which as a new experience enters into the texture of our own mental experience. Understanding is an adventure and, like any other adventure, is dangerous. Just because it is not satisfied with simply wanting to register what is there or said there but goes back to our guiding interests and questions, one has to concede that the hermeneutical experience has a far less degree of certainty than that attained by the methods of the natural sciences. But when one realizes that understanding is an adventure, this implies that it affords unique opportunities as well. It is capable of contributing in a special way to the broadening of our human experiences, our self-knowledge, and our horizon, for everything understanding mediates is mediated along with ourselves.

A further point is that the key terms of earlier hermeneutics, such as the *mens auctoris* or the intention of the text, together with all the psychological factors related to the openness of the reader or listener to the text, are not adequate to what is most essential to the process of understanding to the extent that it is a process of communication. For indeed it is a process of growing familiarity between the determinate experience, or the "text," and ourselves. The intrinsically linguistic condition of all our understanding implies that the vague representations of meaning that bear us along get brought word by word to articulation and so become communicable. The communality of all understanding as grounded in its intrinsically linguistic quality seems to me to be an essential point in hermeneutical experience. We are continually shaping a common perspective when we speak a common language and so are active participants in the communality of our experience of the world. Experiences of resistance or opposition bear witness to this, for example, in discussion. Discussion bears fruit when a common language is found. Then the participants part from one another as changed beings. The individual perspectives with which they entered upon the discussion have been transformed, and so they are transformed themselves. This, then, is a kind of progress — not the progress proper to research in regard to which one cannot fall behind but a progress that always must be renewed in the effort of our living.

The miniature of a successful discussion can illustrate what I have developed in the theory of the fusion of horizons in *Truth and Method,* and it may provide a justification as to why I maintain that the situation of conversation is a fertile model even where a mute text is brought to speech first by the questions of the interpreter.

The hermeneutics that I characterize as philosophic is not introduced as a new procedure of interpretation or explication. Basically it only describes what always happens wherever an interpretation is convincing and successful. It is not at all a matter of a doctrine about a technical skill that would state how understanding ought to be. We have to acknowledge what is, and so we cannot change the fact that unacknowledged presuppositions are always at work in our understanding. Probably we should not want to change this at all, even if we could. It always harvests a broadened and deepened self-understanding. But that means hermeneutics is philosophy, and as philosophy it is practical philosophy.

The great tradition of practical philosophy lives on in a hermeneutics that becomes aware of its philosophic implications, so we have recourse to this tradition about which we have spoken. In both cases, we have the same mutual implication between theoretical interest and practical action. Aristotle thought this issue through with complete lucidity in his ethics. For one to dedicate one's life to theoretic interests presupposes the virtue of *phronesis.* This in no way restricts the primacy of theory or of an interest in the pure desire to know. The idea of theory is and remains the exclusion of every interest in mere utility, whether on the part of the individual, the group, or the society as a whole. On the other hand, the primacy of "practice" is undeniable. Aristotle was insightful enough to acknowledge the reciprocity between theory and practice.

So when I speak about hermeneutics here, it is theory. There are no practical situations of understanding that I am trying to resolve by so speaking. Hermeneutics has to do with a theoretical attitude toward the practice of interpretation, the interpretation of texts, but also in relation to the experiences interpreted in them and in our communicatively unfolded orientations in the world. This theoretic stance only makes us aware reflectively of what is performatively at play in the practical experience of understanding. And so it appears to me that the answer given by Aristotle to the question about the possibility of a moral philosophy holds true as well for our interest in hermeneutics. His answer was that ethics is only a theoretical enterprise and that anything said by way of a theoretic description of the forms of right living can be at best of little help when it comes to the concrete application to the human experience of life. And yet the universal desire to know does not break off at the point where concrete practical discernment is the decisive issue. The connection between the universal desire to know and concrete practical discernment is a reciprocal one. So it appears to me, heightened theoretic awareness about the experience of understanding and the practice of understanding, like philosophical hermeneutics and one's own self-understanding, are inseparable.

Hermeneutics as a Theoretical and Practical Task

Not only the word *hermeneutics* is ancient. The reality designated by the word is as well, whether it be rendered today with such expressions as *interpretation, explication,* *translation,* or even only with *understanding.* At any rate, it precedes the idea of methodical science developed by modernity. Even modern linguistic usage itself reflects something of the peculiar two-sidedness and ambivalence of the theoretical and practical perspective under which the reality of hermeneutics appears. In the late eighteenth as well as in the early nineteenth centuries, the singular emergence of the term *hermeneutics* in certain authors shows that at that time the expression, coming probably from theology, penetrated the general language usage; and then it obviously denoted only the practical capacity of understanding, in the sense of the intelligent and empathetic entry into another's standpoint. It comes up as a term of praise among the pastoral types. I discovered the word in the German author Heinrich Seume (who of course had been a student with Morus in Leipzig) and in Johann Peter Hebel. But even Schleiermacher, the founder of the more recent development of hermeneutics into a general methodological doctrine of the *Geisteswissenschaften,* appeals emphatically to the idea that the art of understanding is required not only with respect to texts but also in one's intercourse with one's fellow human beings.

Thus hermeneutics is more than just a method of the sciences or the distinctive feature of a certain group of sciences. Above all it refers to a natural human capacity.

The oscillation of an expression like *hermeneutics* between a theoretical and a practical meaning is encountered elsewhere too. For example, we speak of logic or its lack in our day-to-day intercourse with our fellow human beings, and by this we are not at all referring to the special philosophical discipline of logic. The same holds true for the word *rhetoric,* by which we designate the teachable art of speaking, as well as the natural gift and its exercise. Here it is altogether clear that without any native endowment the learning of what can be learned leads only to quite modest success. If natural giftedness for speaking is lacking, it can scarcely be made up for by methodological doctrine. Now this will surely be the case as well for the art of understanding, for hermeneutics.

This sort of thing has its significance for the theory of science. What kind of science is it that presents itself more as a cultivation of a natural gift and as a theoretically heightened awareness of it? For the history of science this presents an open problem. Where does the art of understanding belong? Does hermeneutics stand closer to rhetoric? Or should one bring it more in proximity with logic and the methodology of the sciences? Recently I have tried to make some contributions to these questions for the history of science.[1] Like linguistic usage, inquiry into the history of science also indicates that the notion of method, fundamental to modern science, brought into dissolution a notion of science that was open precisely in the direction of such a natural human capacity.

So there arises the more general question as to whether there survives into our own day a sector within the systematic framework of the sciences that is more strongly tied to the earlier traditions of the concepts of science than to the notion of method proper to modern science. It may still be asked whether this is not at least the case for the clearly circumscribable domain of the so-called *Geisteswissenschaften* — and this without prejudice to the question whether a hermeneutic dimension does not play a role in every instance of the desire to know, even that of the modern sciences of nature.

Now there does exist at least one exemplar of the sort pertinent to the theory of science, which could lend a certain legitimacy to such a reorientation of the methodical heightening of awareness on the part of the *Geisteswissenschaften*. This is the practical philosophy established by Aristotle.[2]

Aristotle claimed a peculiar independence for practical philosophy in relation to Platonic dialectics inasmuch as he understood the latter as theoretic knowledge. He opened up a tradition of practical philosophy that exercised an influence right down to the nineteenth century, until it was dissolved in our own century in so-called political science or *Politologie*. Despite all the specificity with which Aristotle sets the idea of practical philosophy against Plato's unified science of dialectics, the aspect of practical philosophy relevant for the theory of science has remained quite obscure. Right down to our own day there have been attempts to see in the method of Aristotelian ethics, which was introduced by Aristotle as practical philosophy and in which the virtue of practical reasonableness (*phronesis*) takes up a central place, nothing more than the exercise of practical rationality. (The fact that any human action lies under the standard of practical rationality and hence also of the contribution of Aristotelian thought on the matter says nothing about the method of practical philosophy.)

It is not surprising that there is dispute about this point because general statements by Aristotle about the methodology and systematic aspects of the sciences are relatively scarce, and when they occur they evidently have the methodological specificity of the sciences less in view than the diversity of their objective fields. This is especially the case for the first chapter of *Metaphysics*, Book Epsilon, and its doublet at K7. There, of course, physics (and in Aristotle's ultimate intention, first philosophy in general) is distinguished as theoretical science from science as practical and poetic. But if one examines how the distinction of theoretical and nontheoretical sciences gets grounded, one discovers that the discussion attends solely to the differences in the objects of such knowing. Now this surely corresponds with Aristotle's general methodological principle that method always must be directed toward its object and what is relevant to its objects. Thus the matter is clear. In the case of physics its object is distinguished by self-movement. In contrast, the object of the productive sciences, the work to be produced, has its source in the producing agent and his knowledge and ability; likewise, what guides the one engaged in practical and political action is determined by the agent and his knowledge. Thus it can appear as if Aristotle were speaking here about technical knowledge (for instance, that of the physician) and about the practical knowledge of one who makes a reasonable decision (*prohairesis*) as though such knowledge itself constituted the practical science that is correlative to the theoretical knowledge of physics. But this is obviously not the case. The sciences being differentiated here (besides which in the theoretical realm there enters the further distinction of physics, mathematics, and theology) are introduced as the sort that strive to know the *archai* and *aitiai* — the principles and determining factors. It is a matter here of inquiry into the *arche* (*Arche-Forschung*); and that means not the knowledge of a physician or a craftsman or a politician that is always to be found in application but knowledge about what may be said and taught in general about such knowing.

It is characteristic that Aristotle does not at all reflect upon this distinction. Obviously for him it is taken for granted that in these realms knowledge of the universal raises no independent claim whatsoever but rather constantly entails being transformed in concrete application to a single case. Yet our consideration of the matter shows that it is necessary to make a sharp distinction between the philosophical sciences, which thematize the practical or poetic performances of acting or producing (including poetry and the "making" of speech), to distinguish the investigation of these performances from the performances themselves. Practical philosophy is not the virtue of practical reasonableness.

Of course one hesitates to apply the modern notion of theory to practical philosophy, which by its own self-characterization already means to be practical. Thus it is a problem of the utmost difficulty to work out the specific conditions of the scientific quality that holds sway in these areas, whereas Aristotle himself characterizes them only with the vague indication that they are less exact. In the case of practical philosophy the state of affairs is particularly complicated, and for this reason it called forth a certain methodological reflection on Aristotle's part. Practical philosophy needs a unique kind of legitimation. Obviously the decisive problem is that this practical science is involved with the all-embracing problem of the good in human life, which is not confined to a determinate area like the other modes of technical knowledge. In spite of this the expression *practical philosophy* intends precisely to say that it makes no determinate use of arguments of a cosmological, ontological, or metaphysical sort for practical problems. Although we are here restricted to the practical good, to what is of importance for human beings, it is still clear that the method for handling these questions of practical action is fundamentally different from practical reason itself.

Already implicit in the apparent pleonasm of a theoretical philosophy, and most specifically in the self-designation practical philosophy, is something mirrored in the reflection of philosophers right down to our own day: that philosophy cannot renounce the claim not merely to know but even to have a practical effect. In other words, as the science of the good in human life, it promotes that good itself. In the case of the productive sciences, the so-called *technai,* this is obvious even for us. They are precisely teachable skills or techniques (*Kunstlehren*) for which practical use alone is the decisive issue. In the case of political ethics, it is completely otherwise, and yet it is hardly possible to repudiate such a practical intent. Thus it has arisen almost always right down to our own day. Ethics does not simply intend to describe valid norms; it wants to ground their validity or even to introduce more adequate norms.

At least since Rousseau's critique of the rationalist pride of the Enlightenment, this has become a real problem. How should the philosophic science of moral affairs legitimate its claim to exist at all if it is true that the undistorted character of natural moral consciousness knows how to recognize the good and duty with unsurpassable exactitude and the most delicate sensitivity? This is not the place to spell out *in extenso* the way Kant grounded the enterprise of moral philosophy in the face of Rousseau's challenge or even to expound the way Aristotle sets himself the same question and tries to do it justice by bringing out the special preconditions set for a student who can meaningfully receive theoretical instruction about the "practical good." Practical philosophy functions in our context only as an example of the tradition of this kind of knowing that does not correspond to the modern notion of method.

Our theme is hermeneutics, and for this theme the relationship of hermeneutics with rhetoric stands in the foreground. Even if we did not know that early modern hermeneutics had been developed as a sort of construction parallel to rhetoric in conjunction with Melanchthon's renewal of Aristotelianism, the problem of rhetoric for a theory of science would be a ready-made point of orientation. Clearly the ability to speak has the same breadth and universality as the ability to understand and interpret. One can talk about everything, and everything one says has to be able to be understood. Here rhetoric and hermeneutics have a very close relationship. The skilled mastery of such abilities in speaking and understanding is demonstrated to the utmost in written usage in the writing of speeches and in the understanding of what is written. Hermeneutics may be precisely defined as the art of bringing what is said or written to speech again. What kind of an art this is, then, we can learn from rhetoric.

What rhetoric as a science is, or what the art of rhetoric consists of, is a problem that was already considered in the initial phases of reflection on the theory of science. It was the well-known antagonism between philosophy and rhetoric in the Greek educational setup that provoked Plato to pose the question concerning the cognitive character of rhetoric. After Plato in his *Gorgias* equated all of rhetoric as an art of flattery with the art of cooking and set it in opposition to any serious knowledge, the Platonic dialogue *Phaedrus* was dedicated to the task of endowing rhetoric with a more profound meaning and of allowing it a share of a philosophical justification. Thus it was asked there exactly what facet of rhetoric is a *techne*. The perspectives laid open in the *Phaedrus* were also at the root of Aristotelian *Rhetoric,* which presents more a philosophy of human life as determined by speech than a technical doctrine about the art of speaking.

Such a notion of rhetoric shares with dialectic the universality of its claim insofar as it is not confined to a determinate realm as usually holds true for the specialized capability of a *techne*.

This is precisely the reason why it could enter into competition with philosophy and rival it as a universal propaedeutic. Now the *Phaedrus* wants to show that when a rhetoric posited with such a breadth wishes to overcome the narrowness of merely rule-governed technique (which according to Plato contains only τὰ πρὸ τῆς τέχνης ἀναγκαῖα μαθήματά, *Phaedrus* 269b), it ultimately has to be taken up into philosophy, into the totality of dialectical knowledge. This process of demonstration is of concern to us here because what is said in the *Phaedrus* about the elevation of rhetoric beyond a mere technique to the status of true knowledge (which Plato, of course, named *techne*) must be allowed to apply to hermeneutics as the art of understanding.

It is a widely accepted view that Plato understood dialectic (that is, philosophy) itself as a *techne* and that he distinguished its uniqueness in contrast to the other *technai* only in the sense that it is the highest form of knowledge, indeed the knowledge of the most sublime thing given for human beings to know, the good (μέγιστον μάθημα). *Mutatis mutandis* the same had to hold true for the philosophic rhetoric called for by him as well and hence ultimately for hermeneutics too. Aristotle was the first to draw that distinction between science, *techne,* and practical rationality (*phronesis*) that was to have such great consequences.

In fact the conception of practical philosophy rests upon the Aristotelian critique of Plato's idea of the good. Only when one looks into the issues more carefully does it become clear (as I have tried to make plausible in a recent investigation)[3] that the question of the good was actually posed as if it were the utmost fulfillment of that same idea of knowledge pursued by the *technai* and the sciences in their own proper fields. But this question is not really fulfilled in a highest learnable science. The supreme objective of inquiry, the good (τὸ ἀγαθόν), comes up constantly in Socratic argumentation in a negative demonstrative function. Socrates refutes the claim of *technai* to be genuine knowledge.

Hermeneutics as a Theoretical and Practical Task

His own knowledge is *docta ignorantia,* and it is not called dialectic for nothing; only that individual knows who is capable
of standing his ground right down to the final speech and
response. Thus — something that is also relevant for rhetoric
— this knowledge can only be *techne* or science it if becomes
dialectic. Only he is truly capable of speaking who has acknowledged that to which he knows how to persuade people as something good and right and thereby is able to stand up for it. This
knowledge of the good and this capability in the art of speaking
does not mean a universal knowledge of "the good"; rather it
means a knowledge of that to which one has to persuade people
here and now and how one is to go about doing this and in
respect to whom one is to do it. Only when one sees the concretization required by the knowledge of the good does one
understand why the art of writing speeches plays such a role in
the broader argumentation. It too can be an art. Plato acknowledges this with his explicitly conciliatory turning to Isocrates;
but only in the eventuality that, beyond realizing the weakness
of the spoken word, one also recognizes the weakness of anything written and is capable of coming to its aid at any time,
just as one would do for all spoken discourse — in the manner
that the dialectician stands toward speech.

This statement has fundamental bearing. Besides all that goes
into knowledge (which ultimately includes everything knowable,
or "the nature of the whole"), real knowledge has to recognize
the *kairos.* This means knowing when and how one is required
to speak. But this cannot be assimilated on one's own by way of
rules and mere learning by rote. There are no rules governing
the reasonable use of rules, as Kant stated so rightly in his
Critique of Judgment.

In Plato this comes out in the *Phaedrus* (268ff) in an amusing
exaggeration: if anyone were to possess only all the physician's
information and rules of thumb without knowing where and

when to apply them, he would not be a physician. Were a tragedian or musician only to have learned the general rules and techniques of his art and yet produced no work using that knowledge, he would not be a poet or musician (280ff). In the same way, the orator has to know all about τά εὐκαιρίαι τε καὶ ἀκαιρίαι (272a₆).

Here one remarks in Plato an overinflation of the model of *techne* as a learnable science in which he stretches supreme knowledge in the direction of dialectics. Neither the physician nor the poet nor the musician knows the good. The dialectician or the philosopher, who really is one and not a Sophist, does not possess a special knowledge, but in his person he is the embodiment of dialectics or of philosophy. Corresponding with this is the way the true political art also emerges in the dialogue *Statesman* as a kind of artistry in weaving, by which one has to weave together opposing factors into a unity (305e). It is embodied in the statesman. In like manner, in the *Philebus* knowledge of the good life comes about as an art of mixing, which the individual in search of happiness has to realize *in concreto*. In a beautiful work, Ernst Kapp has shown this with regard to the *Statesman*, and my own early works as a beginner toward a criticism of Werner Jaeger's construction of the history of the development had similar points in mind with respect to the *Philebus*.[4]

The elaboration of the distinction of theoretical, practical, and productive philosophy, which appears in its initial stages in Aristotle, has to be considered against this background. So too must its status as theory of science be determined. The dialectical overstretching of rhetoric tried out by Plato in the *Phaedrus* is suggestive of a direction. Rhetoric is indissoluble from dialectics; persuasion that is really convincing is indissoluble from knowledge of the true. To the same degree, understanding has to be thought about from the vantage of knowledge. It is a capacity to learn. And Aristotle stresses this as well when he deals with σύνεσις.[5] What is at issue for the truly dialectical rhetorician as well as for the statesman and in the leading of one's own life is the good. And this does not present itself as the *ergon,* which is produced by making, but rather as *praxis* and *eupraxis* (and that means as *energeia*). Accordingly, even though it is supposed to make good citizens, Aristotelian politics does not actually treat education as productive philosophy. Instead Aristotle deals with it just as he handled the doctrine about constitutional forms — as practical philosophy.

It is correct that the Aristotelian idea of a practical philosophy did not live on in its totality but only in its limitation to politics. This was closer to the notion of technique insofar as it intends to mediate a sort of philosophically grounded specialized information into the scientific thought of modernity at least for a while. On the other hand, Greek moral philosophy determined following ages, and especially modernity, less in its Aristotelian than in its Stoic form of expression. Similarly Aristotle's *Rhetoric* remained relatively uninfluential within the tradition of ancient rhetoric. It was just too much philosophy for the masters of the art of speech and for the guidelines toward a masterly art of speaking. But just because of its philosophic character, which, as Aristotle says, linked it with dialectics and ethics (περὶ τα ἤθη πραγματεία, *Rhet.* 1356a$_{26}$), it found its new hour in the age of humanism and of the Reformation.

Precisely the use made of Aristotelian rhetoric by the reformers and especially Melanchthon is relevant for us here. Melanchthon transformed it from the art of making speeches to the art of following discourses with understanding, which means into hermeneutics. Here two elements came together: the new emphasis upon the characteristic of being written and the new cultivation of reading that set in with the invention of the art of book printing and the Reformation's theological turning against the tradition and toward the scriptural principle. The central role of the Holy Scripture for the preaching of the gospel led to its translation into the vernaculars, and at the same time the doctrine of the universal priesthood of all believers gave rise to a use of Scripture that was in need of a new guidance. Wherever laymen took up reading, it was no longer a matter of people directed to an understanding by way of a spoken lecture. No longer did the impressive rhetoric of the jurist, the priest, or a literate elite come to the support of the reader.

We realize ourselves how hard it is to read aloud a text in a foreign tongue or even a difficult text in one's own language on short notice in such a way that one can make good sense of it. If, in a classroom, one asks a beginner to read a sentence aloud — whether it be in German, Greek, or Chinese — it always ends up Chinese whenever one reads aloud what one does not understand. Only when one understands what one is reading can one modulate and introduce a rhythm in such a way that what is meant really comes out.

Thus it was a heightened difficulty, a difficulty with reading in the sense of bringing the Scriptures to speech, that in the modern period raised the art of understanding in its diverse dimensions to a level of methodical self-awareness.

The characteristic of having been written down is something that is not encountered for the first time during our centuries of a general culture marked by reading, whose end we are perhaps approaching in our day. From the outset the hermeneutic task posed by something's having been written down regards not the external technique of the deciphering of written signs so much as the task of correctly understanding meanings fixed in writing. Whenever writing exercises the function of univocal determination and controllable warrant, both the composition and the comprehension of a text originating in this fashion are tasks requiring an exercise of technique, whether one is dealing with tax lists, contracts (which, to the joy of our investigators of language, are sometimes composed bilingually), or religious or other legal documents. So the technical exercise of hermeneutics is based on an age-old practice as well.

The peculiarly hermeneutical dimension of such an exercise makes us aware of what went on in such practice. The reflection upon the practice of understanding can hardly be dissociated from the tradition of rhetoric. And so it was one of the most important contributions of hermeneutics already achieved by Melanchthon to have developed the doctrine concerning the *scopi,* the perspectives. Melanchthon noticed that Aristotle, just as the rhetoricians do at the beginning of their writings, points to the viewpoint under which one has to apprehend their elucidations. It is clearly one thing to have to interpret a law and quite another to have to interpret the Holy Scripture or a "classical" work of poetry. The meaning of such texts is determined not for a neutral understanding but by their own claim to validity.

There were especially two areas in which the problem of interpreting written texts found available a long-standing technical expertise and brought forth a heightened theoretical consciousness: in the interpretation of legal texts, which made up the stock-in-trade of jurists, especially since the codification of Roman Law under Justinian, and in the interpretation of Holy Scripture in the sense of the ecclesiastical dogmatic tradition of the *doctrina Christiana.* The legal and theological hermeneutics of modern times could link up with these.

Even independently of any codification, the task of finding the law and coming up with a verdict contains an inexorable tension that Aristotle had already thematized clearly: the tension between the universality of the valid legal framework, whether codified or uncodified, and the individuality of the concrete case. That a concrete passing of judgment in a legal question is no theoretical statement but an instance of "doing things with words" is almost too obvious to bear mentioning. In a certain sense the correct interpretation of a law is presupposed in its application. To that extent one can say that each application of a law goes beyond the mere understanding of its legal sense and fashions a new reality.

This is similar to the reproductive arts in which one transcends the given work, whether it be notes or a dramatic text, to the extent that new realities are shaped and determined by the performance. In the case of the reproductive arts, however, it still makes sense to say that each performance is based upon a determinate interpretation of the given work, and it clearly still makes sense to discriminate and affirm different degrees of adequacy among the many possible interpretations offered by the performances. At least in the cases of the literary theater and of music, therefore, and in relation to its ideal determinacy, the performance itself is not a mere re-presentation but an interpretation. And so especially in the case of music, it is taken completely for granted that we speak of the interpretation of a work on the part of an artist reproducing it.

In an analogous manner, then, the application of a law to a given legal case seems to me to contain an act of interpretation. This means, however, that each application of legal prescriptions that appears to do justice to the issue at stake both concretizes and clarifies further the meaning of a given law. Max Weber, it seems to me, was completely right when he said, "Prophets alone have been really *consciously* 'creative' in their conduct towards the existing law, in the sense of fashioning new law. For the most part, it is by no means specifically modern, but, from an objective point of view, proper to the most 'creative' legal practitioners that they felt themselves *subjectively* to be no more than mouthpieces for already existing — perhaps often even latently — norms, as their interpreters and appliers, but not as their creators." It accords with the age-old Aristotelian wisdom that the finding of the law always required the enlarging consideration of equity and that the perspective of equity does not stand in contradiction with the law but precisely by relinquishing the letter of the law brings the legal meaning to complete fulfillment for the first time.

On account of the reception of Roman Law, this old problem of finding the law was experienced more sharply in the beginning of the modern period inasmuch as the traditional forms of legal administration were called into question by the new law of the jurists. Hence the jurist's hermeneutics as the doctrine of interpretation had to be accorded a distinctive significance. In the discussion of the early modern age from Budeus to Vico the defense of *aequitas* took up a lot of space. But one might well mention the fact that legal erudition characteristic of the jurist is with good reason called jurisprudence, which means sagacity in legal affairs. The very word itself recalls the heritage of practical philosophy that considered *prudentia* the highest virtue of practical rationality. It is a sign of the loss of an insight into the methodological uniqueness of this legal erudition and its practical determinacy that in the late nineteenth century the expression *legal science* became predominant.[6]

The situation in theology is similar. To be sure, since late antiquity there has been a kind of art of interpretation, and there was even a rather differentiated doctrine of the diverse modes of interpreting the Holy Scriptures. But the variously distinguished forms of scriptural interpretation from the time of Cassiodorus served more as guidelines for making the Holy Scripture useful to the dogmatic tradition of the Church. They were not at all intended by themselves to supply a way of interpreting Holy Scripture for the sake of mediating correct doctrine. On the other hand, with the Reformation's return to the Scripture itself and especially with the spread of Bible reading even outside the guildly tradition of the clerics (which was implicit in the Reformation doctrine of the universal priesthood), the hermeneutical problem became pressing in an altogether different way. The decisive point here is not that one was dealing with the Holy Scripture in texts in foreign tongues, whose adequate translation into the vernacular languages and whose exact understanding brought into play an entire armature of linguistic, literary, and historical information; the decisive factor was rather that by reason of the radicality of the Reformation return to the New Testament and in virtue of the demotion of the Church's dogmatic tradition, the Christian message itself confronted readers with a new, uncanny radicality. This transcends by far the philological and historical aids that were just as necessary for any other old text in a foreign language.

What Reformation hermeneutics turned up and what especially Flacius emphasized was that the very message of the Holy Scripture stood in the way of the natural preunderstanding of human beings. Not obedience toward the law and meritorious works but faith alone — and that means faith in the incredible fact of God's becoming man and in the resurrection — promises justification. To make that convincing in the face of all reliance upon oneself and one's own merits, one's "good works," is what the interpretation of the Holy Scripture demands. As a result, since the Reformation set this in the foreground even more decisively than it had been in the older Christian tradition, the entire form of the Christian worship service becomes confession, empowerment, and call to faith. It rests therefore as much as possible on the correct interpretation of the Christian message. Once the interpretation of Scripture in the sermon entered more and more into prominence in the worship service in the Christian churches, the special task of theological hermeneutics could come to the fore. It did not serve a scientific understanding of Scripture so much as the practice of proclamation by which the good news is supposed to reach the simple person in such a way that he realizes that he is addressed and intended. Consequently application is not a mere "application" of understanding but the true core of understanding itself. So the problematic of application, which was certainly exaggerated to an extreme in pietism, represents not only an essential moment in the hermeneutics of religious texts but makes the philosophic significance of hermeneutic questions as a whole visible; it is more than a methodological instrument.

Hence it meant a decisive step in the unfolding of hermeneutics that in the age of Romanticism hermeneutics was built up into a universally applicable "teachable skill or technique" (*Kunstlehre*) by Schleiermacher and his successors. It was supposed to legitimate the peculiarity of theological science and its equal methodological rights in the garland of the sciences. For Schleiermacher the understanding approach toward others was a natural endowment of his genius, and he could surely be called the most congenial friend during an age in which the cultivation of friendship reached a true high point. And so he had a clear notion that one could not restrict the art of understanding to science alone. Instead it plays a leading role in the sociable life, and if one seeks to understand the words of an intellectually gifted man to which one finds no immediate entry, one makes constant use of this art. One tries to hear between the words of one's intellectual conversation partner just as one sometimes has to read between the lines of texts.

Nevertheless precisely in the case of Schleiermacher the pressure brought to bear by the modern notion of science upon the self-understanding of hermeneutics is made clear. He distinguishes expressly between a laxer and a more rigorous practice of hermeneutics. The laxer practice begins with the assumption that, when confronted with the utterances of another, correct understanding and agreement is the rule and misunderstanding the exception. On the other hand, the more rigorous practice starts with the assumption that misunderstanding is the rule and that only by way of a skillful exertion can one avoid misunderstanding and reach a correct understanding. It is obvious that with this distinction the task of interpretation has been uprooted from the context of intelligent consensus within which the authentic life of understanding gets constantly negotiated. Now it has to overcome a complete alienation. The imposition of an artificial apparatus that is supposed to open up whatever is alien and make it one's own takes the place of the communicative ability in which people live together and mediate themselves along with the tradition in which they stand.

In accord with this universal thematics of hermeneutics opened up by Schleiermacher and especially with his most distinctive contribution — the introduction of psychological interpretation (which would have to enter in alongside the normally used grammatical interpretation) — is the fact that in the work of his successors, the development of hermeneutics into a methodology became determinative in the nineteenth century. Its object is the texts as an anonymous stock, which confronts the researcher. Among the followers of Schleiermacher, Wilhelm Dilthey in particular pursued the hermeneutical foundation of the *Geisteswissenschaften* in order to establish their equal birthright with the natural sciences, inasmuch as he built upon Schleiermacher's accentuation of psychological interpretation. Thus he considered the most proper triumph of hermeneutics to be the interpretation of works of art that raises to consciousness the unconscious production of genius. In relation to artistic works, all the traditional methods of hermeneutcs (the grammatical, historical, aesthetic, and psychological) attain a higher realization of the ideal of understanding only insofar as all these means and methods serve the comprehension of the individual structure as such. Here and especially in the field of literary criticism, the progressive development of Romantic hermeneutics transposes a heritage that right down to its linguistic usage belies a more ancient origin: that of being criticism or, in other words, of discerning the singular structure in its validity and its content and of discriminating it from all that does not match up to its standard. Dilthey's effort was, of course, aimed at extending the notion of method proper to modern science to the task of "criticism" and scientifically elucidating the poetic expression by means of an interpretative (*verstehenden*) psychology. By way of a detour through the history of literature, this development led to the emergence of the expression *literary science* (*Literaturwissenschaft*). It reflects the fading away of an awareness of tradition during the age of scientific positivism in the nineteenth century, which in the areas where German is spoken, gradually increased assimilation to the ideal of modern science even to the point of a change of nomenclature.

If we look back from this overview of the evolution of modern hermeneutics toward the Aristotelian tradition of practical philosophy and the doctrine of a teachable art or skill, we are faced with the question as to how the notable tension in Plato and Aristotle between a technical notion of knowledge and a practical, political notion of knowledge, which includes the ultimate end of human beings, may be made fruitful within the matrix of modern science and theory of science. As far as hermeneutics is concerned it is quite to the point to confront the separation of theory from practice entailed in the modern notion of theoretical science and practical-technical application with an idea of knowledge that has taken the opposite path leading from practice toward making it aware of itself theoretically.

That in so doing the problem of hermeneutics can achieve a stronger clarification than is possible from within the immanent problematic of the doctrines of scientific methodology seems to me to follow from its twofold relationship to the rhetoric that precedes it on the one hand and to Aristotle's practical philosophy on the other. It is hard enough, of course, to determine a place within the theory of science for a discipline like Aristotle's rhetoric. But we have good cause to locate it very much in the vicinity of poetics, and we would be hard put to dispute the theoretic intention of both writings preserved under Aristotle's name. They do not intend to take the place of technical manuals and to aid in a technical sense the arts of speaking and of poetry. Would they, in Aristotle's view, belong at all in series with the art of healing and of gymnastics, which he gladly calls technical sciences in such a context? Did not he himself, even in the place where he really has theoretically elaborated an immense amount of material concerning political knowledge in his *Politics*, enlarge the horizon of problems proper to practical philosophy to such an extent that over and above the manifold of constitutional forms that he studied and analyzed, the question about the best constitution and therewith a practical problematic, the question regarding the good, remained in the forefront? How then would the art of understanding that we call hermeneutics have been situated within the horizon of the Aristotelian way of thinking?

For me it seems instructive here to note the way the Greek word for the act of understanding and for being habitually understanding toward others, *synesis,* tends as a rule to be encountered in the neutral context of the phenomenon of learning and in exchangeable proximity to the Greek word for learning (*mathesis*); but in the framework of Aristotelian ethics it stands for a kind of intellectual virtue. That is no doubt a narrower designation of a word otherwise used by Aristotle as well in a neutral sense, and it corresponds to a similar terminological narrowing of *techne* and *phronesis* in a like context. But it says a lot. "Being habitually understanding toward others," then, is encountered there in the same sense mentioned at the outset of the usual eighteenth-century use of hermeneutics for knowledge of or understanding for the state of people's souls. "Being habitually understanding toward others" means a modification of practical reasonableness, the insightful judgment regarding someone else's practical deliberations.[7] This obviously implies much more than a mere understanding of something said. It entails a kind of communality in virtue of which reciprocal taking of counsel, the giving and taking of advice, is at all meaningful in the first place. Only friends and persons with an attitude of friendliness can give advice. In fact this points right to the center of the questions connected with the idea of practical philosophy, for moral implications are entailed by this counterpart to moral reasonableness (*phronesis*). What he analyzes here in his *Ethics* are virtues, normative notions that always stand under the presupposition of their normative validity. The virtue of practical reason is not to be thought of as a neutral capacity for finding the practical means for correct purposes or ends, but it is inseparably bound up with what Aristotle calls *ethos*. *Ethos* for him is the *arche*, the "that" from which all practical-political enlightenment has to set out.

For analytic purposes, Aristotle distinguishes between ethical and dianoetic virtues and reduces them back to their origin in the so-called parts of the rational soul. But just what is meant by "parts" of the soul and whether they ought not rather to be thought of as two different aspects of the same thing like the concave and the convex are questions Aristotle himself does not fail to ask (*EN* A 13, 1102a, 28ff). Ultimately even these basic distinctions in his analysis of what the practical good for human beings is have to be construed in the light of the methodical intent raised by his practical philosophy as a whole. They do not intend to invade the proper place of practically reasonable decisions, which are required of the individual in any given situation. All his sketchy descriptions of the typical are rather to be understood as oriented toward such a concretization. Even the famous analysis of the structure of the mean between the extremes, which is supposed to be predicated of the Aristotelian ethical virtues, is an empty determination that suggests a great deal. Not merely that they receive their relative content from the extremes, whose profiles possess a far greater determinacy in people's moral convictions and reactions than the praise-worthy mean; it is the ethos of the σπουδαῖος that is being schematically depicted in this way. The ὡς δεῖ and the ὡς ὁ ὀρθὸς λόγος are not evasions relative to a more stringent terminological exigency but pointers to the concretization in which *arete* alone can reach its determinancy. Achieving this concretization is the real concern of one who possesses the virtue of *phronesis*.

In the light of these considerations, the much-discussed introductory description of the task of practical and political philosophy takes on a more precise contour. What Burnet held to be a conscious adaptation on Aristotle's part to the Platonic use of the term *techne* has its true cause in the interference that arises between the "poetic" knowledge of *techne* and the practical philosophy that clarifies the good in sketchy universality and yet is not itself φρόνησις. And here as well πρᾶξις, προαίρεσις, τέχνη, and μέθοδος stand in series and form a continuum of gradual transpositions. But then Aristotle reflects upon the role that the πολιτική is capable of playing in practical life. He compares the intention of such a practically oriented pragmatics with the target being sighted by the archer when he aims at the goal of his hunt. He will more easily hit the mark if he has his target in view. Of course this does not mean that the art of archery consists merely in aiming at a target like this. One has to master the art of archery in order to hit the target at all. But to make aiming easier and to make the steadiness of the direction of one's shooting more exact and better, the target serves a real function. If one applies the comparison to practical philosophy, then one has to begin with the fact that the acting human being as the one who — in accord with his ἦθος — he is, is guided by his practical reasonableness in making his concrete decisions, and he surely does not depend upon the guidance of a teacher. Even so, it can be a kind of assistance in the conscious avoidance of certain deviations that ethically pragmatic instruction is capable of affording inasmuch as it aids in making present for rational consideration the ultimate purposes of one's actions. It is not confined to a particular field. It is not at all the application of a capability to an object. It can work out methods — they are more like rules of thumb than methods — and it can be elevated like an art that one possesses to the stage of genuine mastery. In spite of these things, it is not really "know-how" which like some knowing-how-to-make just chooses its task (on its own or upon request); it is posed precisely in the way that the practice of one's living poses it. Thus the practical philosophy of Aristotle is something other than the putatively neutral specialized knowledge of the expert who enters upon the tasks of politics and legislation like a nonparticipating observer.

Aristotle expresses this clearly in the chapter that forms the transition from the *Ethics* to the *Politics*. Practical philosophy presupposes that we are already shaped by the normative images or ideas (*Vorstellungen*) in the light of which we have been brought up and that lie at the basis of the order of our entire social life. That does not at all suggest that these normative perspectives remain fixed immutably and would be beyond criticism. Social life consists of a constant process of transformation of what previously has been held valid. But it would surely be an illusion to want to deduce normative notions *in abstracto* and to posit them as valid with the claim of scientific rectitude. The point here is a notion of science that does not allow for the ideal of the nonparticipating observer but endeavors instead to bring to our reflective awareness the communality that binds everyone together.

In my own works I have applied this point to the hermeneutic sciences and stressed the way the being of the interpreter pertains intrinsically to the being of what is to be interpreted. Whoever wants to understand something already brings along something that anticipatorily joins him with what he wants to understand — a sustaining agreement. Thus the orator always has to link up with something like this if his persuading and convincing in disputed questions is to succeed.[8] So, too, any understanding of another's meaning, or that of a text, is encompassed by a context of mutual agreement, despite all possible miscomprehensions; and so too does any understanding strive for mutual agreement in and through all dissent. This includes as well the practice of any truly vital science. It, too, is never a simple application of knowledge and methods to an arbitrary object. Only one who stands within a given science has questions posed for him. How much the problems, thought experiences, needs, and hopes proper to an age also mirror the direction of interest of science and research is common knowledge for any historian of science. But especially in the field of the sciences devoted to that understanding whose universal theme is humanity as embedded within traditions does the claim to universality perdure, which Plato had long since laid to the charge of rhetoric. Hence that same neighborly relationship to philosophy holds good for hermeneutics, which had been the provocative outcome of the discussion of rhetoric in the *Phaedrus*.

This does not in any way mean that the methodical rigor of modern science might be either given up or constrained here. The so-called hermeneutical sciences or *Geisteswissenschaften* fall under the same standards of critical rationality that characterize the methodical procedures of all sciences, even though their angle of interest and procedures differ essentially from those of the natural sciences. But they may justly be permitted to invoke the model of the practical philosophy that could also be called politics by Aristotle. It was named the "most architectonic" of sciences by Aristotle insofar as it embraced within itself all the sciences and arts of the ancient system. Even rhetoric belonged to it. So, too, the claim to universality on the part of hermeneutics consists of integrating all the sciences, of perceiving the opportunities for knowledge on the part of every scientific method wherever they may be applicable to given objects, and of deploying them in all their possibilities. But just as politics as practical philosophy is more than the highest technique, this is true for hermeneutics as well. It has to bring everything knowable by the sciences into the context of mutual agreement in which we ourselves exist. To the extent that hermeneutics brings the contribution of the sciences into this context of mutual agreement that links us with the tradition that has come down to us in a unity that is efficacious in our lives, it is not just a repertory of methods (like the methodological doctrine for the philological sciences that was worked out in the nineteenth century from Schleiermacher and Boeckh down to Dilthey and Emilio Betti) but philosophy. It not only accounts for the procedures applied by science but also gives an account of the questions that are prior to the application of every science, just as did the rhetoric intended by Plato. These are the questions that are determinative for all human knowing and doing, the greatest of questions, that are decisive for human beings as human and their choice of the good.

Notes

1. Now in *Kleine Schriften IV: Variationen* (Tübingen: Mohr, 1977), 148–172.

2. When I was speaking on the theme of this essay in Münster in January 1978, I used the opportunity to pay tribute to the memory of my colleague, Joachim Ritter, whose works contain so much that has advanced the issues under discussion.

3. *Die Idee des Guten zwischen Plato und Aristoteles. Sitzungsberichte der Heidelberger Akademie der Wissenschaften* (Heidelberg: C. Winter Universitaetsverlag: 1978).

4. Ernst Kapp, "Theorie und Praxis," *Mnemosyne* 6 (1938):179–194; H.-G. Gadamer, "Der Aristotelische Protreptikos," *Hermes* 63 (1928):138–164; and *Platos dialektische Ethik* (Leipzig: Meiner, 1931; 2d ed., Hamburg: Meiner, 1968).

5. *Nicomachean Ethics,* 211.

6. The origin of the German translation of *jurisprudentia* by legal science (instead of the earlier "legal erudition") may reach as far back as the beginnings of the historical school, to which Savigny and his *Zeitschrift für die historische Wissenschaft* belongs. There both the analogy with historical science and the critique of a dogmatic notion of natural right play a part. Otherwise the possibility always lay ready for accentuating *scientia* more strongly than *prudentia* and for relegating the consideration of equity entirely to the realm of practice.

7. Claus von Bormann, *Der praktische Ursprung der Kritik.* On page 70 of his in other ways highly useful work, the author stands the foundations up on their head, when he wants to ground understanding of others on "critical self-understanding."

8. Here Chaim Perelman and his school, drawing on the experience of jurists, have revived age-old insights into the structure and significance of argumentation as a rhetorical procedure.

On the Natural Inclination of Human Beings Toward Philosophy

We live in an age that would as soon count philosophy among the theological relics of a bygone age or that suspects nothing so much of having a dependence upon secret or unconscious interests as the ideal of pure theory and of knowledge for the sake of knowledge alone. So it is that the Kantian note that rings out in the affirmation of a natural inclination of human beings toward philosophy awakens the resistance of the consciousness of a period that is no longer ready to trust science and the spirit of critical rationality that animates it. Since the technological civilization and the feverish progress with which it has covered the globe has confronted humanity with breathtaking problems of self-destruction in war and peace, the passion for philosophy appears altogether like an irresponsible flight into a world of fading dreams. And shall we now assert that philosophy pertains as essentially to the natural inclinations of humanity as its technical rationality and its practical shrewdness, the collective impact of which hardly seems sufficient to cope with humanity's future tasks? Is there still time for leisure and for leisurely speculation about the insoluble questions that once occupied philosophers and that found their resonance in human minds far and wide?

Does that exist any more? Even in the year 1812 Hegel compared a cultured people without any metaphysics to a temple without the holy of holies. How far behind the times does that seem? Was it not even then an anachronism to deny the dawning of the age of science after Kant's destruction of "dogmatic" metaphysics and his critical justification of the modern empirical sciences, and after the epochal turning point of the French Revolution (that fertile soil of *philosophie positive*). The rapid demise of the Hegelian empire of the absolute Spirit ratifies in an impressive fashion the end of metaphysics, which is tantamount to the promotion of the empirical sciences to the first rank in the kingdom of the thinking mind. Are they capable of filling this position?

To ask this sort of question means examining whether philosophy really does represent a natural inclination of human beings or whether it might not just be an immature phase of the knowing spirit that had not yet been liberated enough toward its own rationality. This, therefore, is the critical question for philosophy.

What we call philosophy, using a Greek word for a Greek concern, itself means "science." And this Greek concern is presented as *the* decisive phase of the history of humanity by which the West took its leave of the mythology of the primitive period of humanity and set out upon the path of the human desire to know.

Has this path arrived at its goal and philosophy come to an end? Or is it a perduring inclination of the human being that characterizes him as essentially as his knowledge of his death and the fact that he buries his dead? And is it the thought of a beyond that in the West has taken the path of a science of a beyond in relation to nature, the path of metaphysics? What was its beginning? All beginnings lie in the darkness, and what is more, they can be illuminated only in the light of what came later and from the perspective of what followed. Words lead us further back into the darkness of primitive times than any other testimony. What does the word *philosophy* teach us? We know from Plato that he endowed the word with a trenchancy according to which *philosophy* means the incessant though constantly unfulfilled striving after truth, whereas knowing is reserved for the gods. There is no doubt, however, that this is the specifically Platonic imprint upon a more general sense of the word. Thucydides puts in the mouth of Pericles the statement that the Athenians philosophize and love what is beautiful (*philosophoumen kai philokaloumen*). Here the word means "interest in theoretical questions," for "beautiful" refers to the domain of that which surpasses the necessary and useful and is sought for its own sake just because it is pleasing. But as an anecdote about Pythagoras teaches us, the word is obviously a more recently shaped term for theoretic interest in general, and it connects this interest or predilection with the word *wise*, which was used to designate the extraordinary character of men whose knowledge or ability stands out above that of everyone else. Indeed in this word *wise* a semantic coinage was achieved that prepares the way for the Platonic concept *philosophia*. For instance, Heraclitus uses the expression *the wise* for what stands above and behind what we can know and recognize, just as the master stands above his apprentices and above everything that can be learned.

That which is wise, the one wise thing about which Heraclitus wants to inform us and which ought to be displayed in everything as the true, the *logos* common to all things, the cosmic law, universal ground, and universal meaning, the union of being and thinking — this is contrasted just as much with poetic-mythic doctrines of a Homer or a Hesiod as with the Ionian science (whose curiosity about the world and pleasure in inquiry was established as something quite new in comparison with mythic thought). And perhaps indeed even what Hesiod depicts for us as the primal history of the gods and especially what Homer portrays for us as the lives and deeds of the gods is already the free lucidity of poetic imagination and theological systematics rising out of the mythic daybreak. In any case, the obscure, oracular knowledge of Heraclitus — just like the Pythagorean knowledge of cosmos, of numbers, and of souls or Parmenides's logic of being that flies in the face of all sense appearance — is established in contrast with all opinionated knowingness. And this happens under the new claim of *logos,* or reason joining everyone together and raising everything to communicative clarity.

It appears that it was this complex development that elicited from Plato the transformation of the commonly used *philosophia.* He gave it a new orientation critical of the knowledge of his time and at the same time transfigured the man who exercised a decisive influence upon his life and led him to become the first teacher of philosophy and the first founder of a school of philosophy — Socrates. He portrays him as a simple citizen of Athens to whom the knowledge of "the wise people" who investigated nature promised nothing. Instead he advised concern about one's own soul, and he asked the question about the right way to live. He was really a philosopher in the new Platonic sense of the word — not a knower and a wise man but distinguished by knowledge about his own and everyone else's ignorance concerning what is most important and most essential, the good. As tradition has it, he brought philosophy down from heaven — that is, from the inquiry into the structure of the cosmos and of the events of nature down among men, inquiring in restless and tireless conversation about the good. He became the prototype and exemplar for all who see in the philosopher a person concerned about self-knowledge and helped by his thinking to rise above the hard experiences, misfortune, injustice, and suffering of life, indeed above the bitterness of death.

Here a new thread is woven into the cloth out of which the philosopher's mantle has been sewn. The heritage of Socrates, the orientation toward practical wisdom about life independent of science — beginning with Diogenes in his barrel, who knew of nothing more lofty to request of Alexander the Great than that he should stand out of the way of the sun's light — has since run alongside the royal road of Western philosophy. We will meet up with it again.

Plato's way of following Socrates, on the other hand, was not this sort of thing alone. He opened the royal road upon which philosophy in the West became the *regina scientiarum*, the highest of all the sciences. What he practiced in developing further the Socratic art of dialogue was directing dialectic as the supreme and ultimate demand for an account and a foundation, not only (as Socrates had) against the human ignorance of the statesmen, the rhetoricians, and the poets, as well as against those who really understood their crafts, but in the end even against science itself, and that above all was mathematics. What gave dialectic the rank of authentic knowledge was its striving to ground at a deeper level what was proven with the intuitive evidence of mathematical theorems, to reduce surface and figure to number, and that, in turn, to its elements, unity and plurality. For Plato unity and plurality together constitued the ultimate secret of all order, whether of divine or human things, of the cosmic structure and the regime, or of the structure of the soul and of the discourse that issues in thought.

According to Plato, the beginning of philosophy, the desire for knowledge, is wonder (*thaumazein*). It always intervenes at a point where something strikes us as alien because it runs counter to habitual expectations — for example, that numbers and quantities are demonstrably relative and not fixed qualities of things, an experience that calls for insight into numbers and quantities, for mathematics. "Let no one enter here who is ignorant of mathematics" was the inscription above the entrance of the Academy in Athens, the first philosophic school in the West.

Wonder, however, is not only being astonished but also admiration, which means constantly looking up to what is exemplary. The Platonic ascent to the good is the only thing that gives wonder its fulfillment. To Plato, not only mathematics seemed to be in need of foundations but all our knowledge, expert or general, on the basis of which we make our practical decisions. All that requires knowledge of the good.

In this sense, Plato can say of the idea of the good that it is the highest object of knowledge in general. And if Aristotle, too, elaborated this thinking in the direction of a final cause in his first philosophy, he did not connect it integrally with the practical question about the good in human life, but he still shares fully with Plato the cognitive ideal of pure contemplation that proceeds toward a highest knowledge beyond all the sciences.

As we know very well, the modern empirical sciences succeeded only in being liberated from the fetters of the comprehensive knowledge of Aristotelian philosophy by means of arduous critical labor. They purchase the certitude and controllability of their knowledge and the secure path of their progress by renouncing comprehensive knowledge in the grand Aristotelian style. Inasmuch as it subjected what is observable to the quantifying methods of mathematics, empirical science discovered a new notion of natural law and it moved forward to scientific knowledge in all directions by means of experiment and hypothesis.

What the old science, crowned by metaphysics, had provided was a whole orientation to the world, which brought the natural experience of the world and its linguistically mediated interpretation of the world to a unified conclusion. Modern science could not provide this. Just as man no longer considers himself the center of the universe, so too his knowledge is no longer the natural expansion of his experience of the world. Instead it is an independent setup, indeed an attack upon nature, which it subjects to a new but only partial mastery. Philosophy's centuries-long spinning away at the old questions of metaphysics may, since Hume and Kant, have increasingly become a thing of the past; but can the new empirical sciences, which offer no such comprehensive knowledge but a never-ending process of inquiry into nature take the place of philosophy? Could they even pose the questions that unceasingly stir our desire to know, questions that truly spring from wonder? Is not wonder itself still more than Plato's astonishment and admiration? Does it not come to me above all in the face of the alien and the strange? And does that not include everything "strange": the beginning of all things, their duration, and their end? Is there really time at all, or is it merely in us? Why is there anything at all and not nothing? And what is consciousness and self-consciousness, in which everything exists once again? How should we understand that this self-illuminating luminosity that we call consciousness will eventually come to an end? How should anyone who thinks this understand it? Or even that the freedom that he supposes he possesses within himself and that enables him to think beyond spaces and times and eternities is a mere illusion and dream and that it is dominated by something else, a bundle of drives and unconscious pressures? All these considerations come upon us with a qualitatively different degree of strangeness than the enigmatic fact that made Plato's "Theatetus" dizzy — that the same thing is at one and the same time both large and small.

It is characteristic that the prevalence of science as the determinative mark of the age has put an end to the classical function of philosophy, but it has not managed to hinder its survival in a changed form. The nineteenth century was the age of *Weltanschauungen,* a word that in its original semantic content renewed the promise of an interpretation of the whole that science could no longer supply. It is only in resisting this world view thinking that philosophy, in adhering to its task of remaining scientific, turned more and more into a philosophy of science, of its logical and epistemological foundations.

In contrast, art entered in on the side of the philosophy of world views. With the end of metaphysics, the age-old struggle between philosophy and poetry flared up anew. If Plato, in the face of the demand to give an account, which he saw embodied in Socrates, burned his own poems and banned the poets of the Greeks, Homer and the tragedians, from his educational state, now the proper truth claim of art emerged in manifold forms. It is no exaggeration to say that we find the great novels of the nineteenth and twentieth centuries, together with the other kinds of art works from this epoch of bourgeois culture, closer to the old tasks of philosophy and look upon them as the custodian of philosophy's great heritage.

Correspondingly there is in the German-speaking countries a development and function of the so-called *Geisteswissenschaften*, which for their part carry on the heritage of metaphysics. In the area of French culture, philosophy is grouped with *lettres* — so strongly felt is its proximity to poetry that a single word embraces both philosophy and literature. In Anglo-Saxon tongues the old humanistic concept of the *humaniora* has been transferred into their linguistic context under the title "humanities." This is to proclaim that in these sciences, what is made an objective of study is not the world of objects but man's knowledge about himself and the world of his creations in which he has deposited this knowledge.

The aim of these kinds of science is not just knowledge but the vital and ongoing shaping of man's knowledge of himself. From the standpoint of the theory of science, however, all this — the truth claim of art as well as the claim of the *Geistewissenschaften* to serve man's self-understanding — is labelled hybrid, an inadmissible fusion of imagination with the rigor of pure science.

Today in fact, in the age of a new, radicalized faith in science, the role of art in society is just as contested as is the interest in the historical tradition of human culture nurtured by the *Geisteswissenschaften*. There is a new note of expectation with which public awareness turns to science. To be sure, the growing mastery of natural processes still involves a relatively small realm of nature, however decisive for life especially the mastery of energy problems may be in keeping man's house on earth. The weather is a constantly present manifestation of unpredictability, not to mention the terrifying complex of problems that arose with the industrial revolution in respect to the self-endangering of life on this planet, a problem complex that often looks to us like the deadline of human history. But this state of affairs engenders the mounting expectation that science is ultimately capable of banishing all unpredictability from the life most proper to society by subjecting all spheres of human living to scientific control. There is, for example, the mastery of the problems associated with the cultivation of hereditary factors and breeding, as well as the problems of preventing and fighting against disease, which of course can never eliminate the alien character of death. But even the natural foundations of human being in our vital instincts are supposed to be subjected to scientific control; and a harmony between unconscious drives and conscious motivations is supposed to be brought about scientifically. This is the universal claim of contemporary psychoanalysis. Then there are the scientific problems posed by the economy and prosperity, which we expect economics to bring under control. There is the problem of the linguistic consensus among human beings. Not only the multitude of languages men speak but also the inexactitude in the usage of each language and all the problems of understanding and miscomprehension are supposed to be resolved by a new scientific control over language in general, by its rational construction and organization. There are processes of politics, of social life, of the selection of information, of the formation of public opinion, of the conduct of war and peace, that are supposed to be freed from the emotional capriciousness. Finally there is the claim to know the objective course of history, which means of making it humanly manipulable, and that leads in turn to the claim of scientifically planning and producing a science of the future.

The successes of science remain far behind such expectations and hopes in all these realms. For the most part they represent nothing more than frameworks whose filling in and adaptation to changing situations with the means of science does not seem possible. Hence they offer us a certain suggestiveness. But what makes them so popular is something else. The authority of science and of experts adds up to relieving the responsibility that should be borne by the one acting, even though science often cannot give real security. There is no question that extrarational factors play into and have their effect, factors that are more akin to that earlier need connected with the desire to know, which philosophy once encompassed within itself: horizons of expectation and conventions, imaginative representations of what is believed, normative concepts defined by the tradition, and everything that through the ages supports and determines the practical decisions of human beings. In spite of the fact that this is so, it does not of itself decide the legitimacy of the aim of assigning all decisions to the responsibility of science. To enable us to decide this question, one has to envisage perfect control of all these spheres of life and wonder. Could such a control satisfy our desire to know — not least, the desire to know what we have to do? Would it be possible to conceive and to will such a completely scientific control of the life of the individual as well as of the life of the society that every personal and political decision would be decided objectively — not by ourselves but by science? Or is our desire to know the sort that constantly needs to be nourished from other sources than those of a research making ever further progress? Is it not crucial to man's knowledge of himself that he, like Socrates, knows what he does not know, and never shall know? Should the questions to which science does not know the answer be shunted aside even though they still concern the human mind and have called forth the grand answers of the religions, the mythologies, artistic creations like the tragedies, and intellectual works like the Platonic dialogues?

No one would hold the opinion that in the face of these old questions and of that new orientation of science, philosophy should once again take over its old comprehensive function and that it could integrate all our knowledge within a unified image of the world. But the natural inclination of human beings toward philosophy, toward the desire to know, prevails. Are we not still faced with the task of transposing into our practical consciousness both the knowledge of science (limited and provisional, or verified and efficacious as it may be) and all the knowledge of man that streams toward us out of the great historical tradition? Here I see the challenge to authentic integration: to join together science and man's knowledge of himself in order to achieve a new self-understanding of humanity. We badly need this, for we live in a condition of ever-increasing self-estrangement, which, far from being caused by the peculiarities of the capitalist economic order alone, is due rather to the dependence of our humanity upon that which we have built around ourselves as our civilization.

Thus the task of bringing people to a self-understanding of themselves takes on an intense urgency. Philosophy has served this task for ages. It has done so as well in the form of philosophy that I name hermeneutics (the theory and also the practice of understanding and bringing to language the alien, the strange, and whatever has become alien). This may help us to gain our freedom in relation to everything that has taken us in unquestioningly, and so especially with respect to our own capabilities. In the end, Plato remains correct. Only by the demythologization of science (which controls what is proper to it but cannot know the one whom it serves) can the mastery of knowledge and ability become self-mastery. The Delphic demand "Know thyself" meant, "Know that you are a man and no god." It holds true as well for human beings in the age of the sciences, for it stands as a warning before all illusions of mastery and domination. Self-knowledge alone is capable of saving a freedom threatened not only by all rulers but much more by the domination and dependence that issue from everything we think we control.

Philosophy or Theory of Science?

My suggested topic has an odd ring to it. As if the theory of science (*Wissenschaftstheorie*) were not philosophy as well. The intention of the question posed then must be, Can there still be such a thing as philosophy in any form other than that of theory of science? Is the age of philosophy over, in the sense that with the death of Hegel (1831) the age of metaphysics was over and done? In the age of science in which we are living, is not the only legitimate sense of philosophy that of the theory of science? Was it not precisely the undoing of the development of philosophy in our century, in the time of the decline of Neo-Kantianism, that under the popular name of existential philosophy it separated from science and took upon itself a unique claim?[1]

In fact it used to be the scientific claim of philosophy to steer clear of its surrogate, world views. Philosophy itself was supposed to be a rigorous science. Under the banner of the rediscovery of Kant in the second half of the nineteenth century, this was taken for granted. In a characteristic narrowing of sights, one appealed in this regard to Kant and in particular to the accessible form he had given the critical philosophy in his so-called *Prologomena*.[2] To be sure, this writing was intended only to provide a more convenient presentation of the basic idea of the *Critique of Pure Reason,* but it actually brought about the genuine breakthrough and astonishingly swift victory of the idea of critical philosophy in the 1780s. Whoever reads it today discovers with a certain surprise that the epistemological interpretation of Kant developed in the later nineteenth-century return to Kant could appeal with a certain justice to the Kant of the *Prologomena*. Here it really sounds almost as if the fact of science were presupposed and that the Kantian critique intended nothing more than the legitimating justification for this fact. Indeed this was the perspective in terms of which *Erkenntnistheorie* (epistemology) rose to become the fundamental discipline of philosophy, and the *Critique of Pure Reason* was drawn completely within the perspective of epistemology. This was expressed in the fact that the French and the English equivalent for the concept of *Erkenntnistheorie* that arose in the nineteenth century was *epistemologie* or "epistemology." These words let the Greek expression for science, and so the equation of all knowledge with scientific knowledge, resonate. The object of knowledge, Kant's famous "thing-in-itself," is, as it was expressed in the formulation of Marburg Neo-Kantianism, nothing but an "infinite task," and that means "for scientific research."

It could not be long before the framework of transcendental reflection that grasped the conditions of the possibility of experience in terms of the foundations of the empirical sciences was extended to the whole sphere of culture. So within Neo-Kantianism itself, and especially in its southwest German form, there emerged, besides the categories constitutive of the object of knowledge, the substitute notion of values whose validity it would be the task of transcendental reflection to justify, just as the basic theoretic concepts of knowledge were grounded in the so-called epistemology. In this way the *Geisteswissenschaften* came up with a transcendental grounding analogous to the epistemological justification of the natural sciences. It was the value reference that supposedly defined the concept of the historical fact.

The return to Kant or Neo-Kantianism in the variety of its
types was only one of the dominant tendencies of the age. The
other was the so-called empiricist orientation that became thoroughly influential in the German-speaking world by way of
English inductive logic, especially that of John Stuart Mill.[3]
Empiricism refers to the derivation of the validity of our concepts from their link with the primary contents of experience
that attain their givenness in sense perception. Here empirical
science was not only a fact in need of grounding; the grounding
of science and its universal concepts itself was understood as a
way and a work of experience. But whether in the shape of
transcendental apriority or of logical empiricism, both positions
understood themselves in the light of the dissolution of dogmatic metaphysics, whether this went back to Kant or Hume,
and they corresponded completely with the characterization of
the age which August Comte's construction of the history of
philosophy had designated as the age of positive science in
contrast to the age of metaphysics.[4]

The word *positive* is vague enough. The situation of philosophy at the start of our century is distinguished by the way it
could understand itself as a battle over the true positivism and
thus, in the end, as a justification of the positive sciences. The
concept of the positive or of the given was itself indeterminate
and ambiguous. Givenness is givenness for . . . That evidently
means givenness for consciousness. But does that also mean, as
the early positivism had asserted, that the only things given for
consciousness, to which all knowledge of the external world may
be reduced, are sense givennesses, that is, the so-called sense
data, so that it is ultimately a mechanics of sensations that lies
at the basis of the structure of our experiential world? This is
where criticism intervenes. Does sensation as a real givenness in
consciousness exist at all? Or does the degree to which sensations
can claim validity as building blocks of knowledge depend in

the end upon what consciousness itself intends and knows when one experiences something as given? But what are data for consciousness? Can the validity of our concepts (and even if only in the field of logic) be comprehended on the basis of the psychological investigation of our consciousness?

It was the devastating critique of the distortions that sensualistic psychology had produced especially in regard to logical structures that led to a new, more profound grounding of apriority in philosophy: the phenomenology of Edmund Husserl.[5] The victorious reproval of psychologism in the first volume of the *Logical Investigations* was still only the first step toward a new philosophical foundation. The Neo-Kantian orientation of transcendental reflection was opened up and broadened to an immense field of phenomenological inquiry, which proposed to study the correlation of differentiated modes of consciousness, the so-called intentionalities, with the intentional objects correlative to them.

In the concept of intentionality, the dogmatically posited split between the immanence of self-consciousness and the transcendence of one's knowledge of the world, which lay at the root of the notion of epistemology and its theoretic constructions, was fundamentally overcome. Epistemology was transformed into the phenomenology of knowledge, and philosophy into phenomenology, insofar as the latter grounded the constitution of all objective validity in the intentional accomplishments of consciousness. However, the older sensualistic grounding of knowledge, which for its part was called "positivism," no longer adhered to the dogmatic concept of sensory givenness; instead it began to investigate the question about the foundations of knowledge — prescinding from all physiological-psychological preoccupations — as if it could find its justification in the pure immanence of the truth claim of statements. Its theoretic work was devoted to the problematic of protocol statements, for these were held to be statements about whose truth no possible doubt can arise because the expression of the statement coincides with the immediate experience of an observable state of affairs. From this basis the logical structure of the world was supposed to be attained.[6]

Thus both philosophic apriority and logical empiricism raise the same universal claim to ground the totality of possible knowledge — and that meant to justify the claim of science. But it was also the case that such styles of scientific philosophy could not embrace within themselves and justify as scientifically grounded all that belonged to the philosophical sciences in the classical tradition of the West. Let us recall what kind of knowledge that was. Everyone is familiar with that tradition under the name of metaphysics, and everyone knows as well that this name does not actually come up in the founder of the tradition, Aristotle, but that it was called "first philosophy" (*prima philosophia*) instead. What most people do not usually realize is the implication of this designation: that as long as philosophy represented the comprehensive title for every kind of theoretical knowledge and science, first philosophy could be a meaningful designation only for the question about what is first, the principle. The first philosophy was not only the first among the philosophic sciences but first among all the sciences, which in general are encompassed in the *Summae* of the Greek-Christian tradition. Philosophy means "science."

If one wishes to understand the problematic relationship between philosophy and science that prevails at the present time, one has to begin by acknowledging the profound and incisive significance of the seventeenth century. At that time a new idea of science developed and found its first theoretical grounding. With Galileian mechanics and the spread of its procedures into the entire field of experience a new idea of science emerged. It was independent of the foundation of first philosophy, the doctrine of substance as the true being. The bold enterprise of a mathematical description and analysis of phenomena, which left the evidence of visible appearance behind and led Galileo to the establishment of the laws of mechanics, was expressly purchased by renouncing any knowledge of substances. Galileo subjected nature to mathematical construction and so achieved a new notion of natural law. Inquiry into the laws of nature on the basis of mathematical abstraction and its verification by means of measuring, counting, and weighing were present at the birth of the modern sciences of nature. They made possible for the first time the complete application of science to the technical transformation of nature for humanly conceived purposes. And this has marked our civilization on a planetary scale.

It was especially the idea of method, or of securing the path of knowledge in accord with the guiding ideal of certainty, that brought a unified meaning of knowing and knowledge to the fore. This meaning no longer stood in the taken-for-granted context of the tradition of our earlier knowledge of the world. This is the first presupposition underlying the present question. The new conception of science grounded for the first time the narrower sense of philosophy that we have connected with the word *philosophy* since then.

Of course it was not just a matter of exclusion but of a confrontation, even of a union of the earlier idea of science with the later. From now on, this was the "proper" task of "philosophy." The first telling example for this sense of the philosophical sciences that dominated modern thinking until Kant and Hegel is reflected most clearly in the works of Descartes.[7] His *Discourse on Method,* and still more the elaboration of his ideal of method in the so-called *Regulae,* which first came to light in 1700, long after his death, was meant to develop a novel ideal of knowledge. At the same time it intended to be accountable to the cognitive claim of the tradition. Descartes' most well-known work expresses this self-accountability in the title: the *Meditations on First Philosophy* does not so much mean that here a new foundation for philosophy has been moved into the place of the old (as is suggested by the German translation) but, to the contrary, that the new ideal of cognition and method had to seek its grounding and justification in the "old" truths. It was something monstrous that Descartes in his radical treatment of doubt called into question the totality of our intelligible world in its legitimacy and discovered a final certitude only in the unshakability of explicit self-consciousness. And he did this not the way the ancient skepticism did with its antidogmatic tenor but for the sake of grounding and justifying a new, methodical way of knowledge. It was obvious to him that one can find the guarantee for the application of rational truths to the world of experience not merely in the indubitability of self-consciousness alone but in the idea of God that found its evident demonstration in that self-consciousness. Precisely this seemed to Neo-Kantianism and, in another way, even to Husserl as nothing but a lack of clarity and of coherence, so greatly had the task of metaphysics been deflated in the meantime. In truth, for Descartes the whole point of his new reflection upon the truths of metaphysics lay in the fact that only against the background of this old notion of truth and of this divine guarantor could the new science be grounded.

Thus Descartes stands at the beginning of the age of the great philosophic systems, which, taken together, all had as their task and their distinctiveness that they joined together what is incompatible and sought to integrate into the totality of our experience of the world what was becoming ever more fragmented in the particularity of scientific research. That is the meaning of a "system" of philosophy, which emerged then and right down to our own day betrays an uncritical access to the subject matter or concerns of philosophy.

The great model of the Leibnizian synthesis of universal mathematics and a metaphysics of individuality defines the meaning of philosophy precisely in the sense that it mediated the new idea of science with the tradition of metaphysics. If one sees Kant's own critical performance in the context of this more general task of the later philosophy, then one notes that it looks to be something quite different from what the Neo-Kantian justification of the fact of science by transcendental reflection suggested. However much Kant objects to the Leibnizian synthesis and the ideal of knowledge by way of concepts alone as "dogmatic metaphysics" and however much he refuted that project by means of his *Critique,* he still certainly understands himself within the metaphysical horizon of questioning. It is not just that his moral philosophy posits the essential contents of traditional metaphysics as newly valid on the basis of the rational fact of freedom. But even the notion of a metaphysics of nature (of a purely rational science that would unfold the basic concepts of nature) still holds meaning for him. However, the bold attempts of Kant's successors to raise the experiential a posteriori factor and the rational a priori factor to the point of perfect identity fastened completely upon the idea of metaphysics and undertook for the last time the derivation of the unity of the philosophic sciences as the unity of all knowledge.[8]

Remaking physics into a speculative physics (which meant encompassing the multifaceted progress of knowledge of nature within a philosophy of nature claiming conceptual necessity and subordinating the endless field of historical experience to the necessity of the spirit conceiving itself) was an attempt surely doomed to failure. But philosophic reason still faces the task of joining together all knowledge into a whole. Does that not have to mean acknowledging in nature and spirit and history the realizations of one and the same "reason"? It is not an accident that Hegel developed the basic discipline of the philosophical sciences, the transcendental logic, out of the Greek concept of the *logos*.[9] As the great renewer of the Platonic dialectic, he confessed his allegiance to the Greek beginnings of a philosophic and scientific tradition, which even in the age of science demonstrate their inexhaustible vitality. It is the turn to the communicatively understood and intelligible world, which the Platonic Socrates had designated as the second-best journey, the flight to the *logoi*,[10] which Hegel still takes as well. To understand the world in the same way one understands one's own behavior when he has known something as "good": in this thought-worthy self-justification, put by Plato in the mouth of Socrates as he awaited his execution, an understanding of the world was legitimated that does not, to be sure, correspond to our notion of science, but it is also not to be eliminated by thought from our own experience of the world.

The age of science, which began its course after the breakdown and end of the Hegelian synthesis of philosophy and science, is no longer capable of fully encompassing in itself the heritage of this tradition. That is what lies at the root of the question, Philosophy or theory of science? In the age of science, is there any way of preserving and validating the great humane heritage of knowledge and wisdom?

That it cannot be done by any sheer restoration was shown especially by the loss of public significance undergone by philosophy in the course of the nineteenth century. It was the great outsiders like Schopenhauer and Nietzsche, and not Hermann Lotze or Eduard Zeller (the inventor of the term, *Erkenntnistheorie* [cognitional theory as epistemology]), who determined the nineteenth century.[11] Then the word *Weltanschauung* ("world view") evolved into a fashionable term, a true *plurale tantum*; the very word brings to expression the relativity of *Weltanschauungen*. They appealed to science but precisely did not allow of full scientific verification. To this migration into

Weltanschauung thinking, with its indissoluble plurality, corresponded the unfolding of historical consciousness. Wilhelm Dilthey,[12] the philosophical proponent of the historical school, considered the task of philosophy to be the grounding of the plurality of *Weltanschauungen* in the "thought-forming labor of life." This meant that for the entirety of the interpretation of the world, which the world views offered, philosophy was no longer taken seriously in its claim to knowledge; instead it had a validity like that of the other cultural creations of humanity (such as art, law, and religion) as an expression of life, which was capable of becoming an object of scientific knowledge but insofar as it is an expressive phenomenon is not itself knowledge. The thought form for this scientific treatment of *Weltanschauungen* was typology. Behind this, however, there lay concealed the fundamental objection of historical relativism, which no sort of argumentative art was able to resolve and which was directed against any claim of philosophy to be knowledge derived from concepts.

We have thereby arrived at the situation from which the estrangement between philosophy and science in the twentieth century derives. Certainly one could designate and claim as the task of philosophy comprehension of the falling apart of human thought into types of *Weltanschauung.* In particular, this was the achievement of *Existenzphilosophie,* which developed out of the experience of limit situations (in which the knowledge of science could no longer furnish any real orientation) a unique concept of existence, in the sense of a thematization of the reasonableness of existence. In doing so, however, the sciences were allowed to stand on their own in their compelling correctness and were removed from the foundational claim of philosophy; on the basis of the conditionedness of existence, the latter undertook to read the ciphers of transcendence — as metaphysics, as religion, and as art — and thereby philosophy was pushed into the light of the private sphere.

It is not the universal significance of science for human civilization that resists such a privatizing of philosophy; it could be its destiny only to maintain itself in a retreat into the private. Nevertheless the social function of science and its making possible of technology is not something external in relation to which philosophy could enjoy an unperturbed reign over the kingdom of interiority and of reasonable freedom. Especially the increasing significance of science for the technique of forming opinion and judgment within human society forbids an appeal to the reason of *Existenz* at the margins of the scientific world orientation. Not to be able to do this any longer is the signature of our age. Even though philosophy has to restrain itself from intervening in the work of the sciences in a directive or corrective fashion, it has now for the first time to turn itself toward its old task of giving an account for our life as shaped by science. The independence of science from philosophy means at the same time its irresponsibility — not in the moral sense of the word but in the sense of its incapacity and its lack of any perceived need to give an account of what it itself means within the totality of human existence, or especially in its application to nature and society. That of course is not what the so-called theory of science regards as its task. But if it really intends to be a giving of accounts, should it not go beyond the task of an immanent justification of the doing of science? Should its giving of accounts not aim at the totality of knowledge, and science within this totality of knowledge? and then does it not run up against the questions that philosophy has always asked and cannot give up asking — neither after Kant's critique "that corrodes everything" nor after the discrediting of "speculation" in the nineteenth century, nor even after the verdict that the ideal of the "unity of science" had hurled upon all "metaphysics"?

I would like to show that it is not merely a universal a priority that has need of inquiring behind science, but that there is implied in every theory of science itself the idea of self-justification, which compels it to go beyond itself. Hence it was a peculiarity of phenomenology in contrast to the other forms of Neo-Kantianism that it undertook to elucidate the constitutive concepts of the natural experience of the world that still antecedes scientific methodology. The recent coining of the word *Lebenswelt* ("life world"), which played such an important role in the philosophic giving-of-accounts in the work of the later Husserl, is a clear expression of this.[13] But phenomenology came up against a limit for its ideal of "final grounding." The *aporiai* connected with the self-referential character of phenomenology as the science of pure consciousness and especially the *aporiai* connected with the self-constitution of temporality, in which the transcendental self-consciousness of the ego entangles itself, brought the entire project of a transcendental phenomenology to its downfall.

Heidegger's critique of the notion of consciousness and his disclosure of its ontological predisposition constituted the crucial breakthrough in this matter.[14] That was the real point of the introduction to the question of being (*Seinsfrage*) that *Being and Time* offers. If Heidegger took it upon himself to pose anew the question about being (*Sein*), it was only a matter of consistency that ultimately the temporality of human *Dasein* (its finitude and historicality) that opened up the horizon of the question of being did not simply take the place of transcendental consciousness; rather the complete thought form of a transcendental grounding collapsed. To be sure it was already a meaningful insight that the notion of scientific objectivity may be understood ontologically as a derivative mode of human *Dasein* and its way of being in reference to the world. Only fools could see in such an ontological derivation a diminishment of the significance or legitimacy of science. It could still appear, however, as if philosophy's radical way of putting the question would unilaterally assign the legitimate business of science its place. In truth, it was exactly the point of the ontological insight mediated by Heidegger's thought that science originates from an understanding of being that compels it unilaterally to lay claim to every place and to leave no place unpossessed outside of itself. But that means that today not metaphysics but science is dogmatically abused.

A similar criticism of dogmatic presuppositions, however, was accomplished in the field of logical empiricism itself. If the apodictic evidence of self-consciousness was revealed by the Heideggerian critique of phenomenology to be an ontological prejudice, so the conception of logical empiricism had a dogmatic element too, which lay especially in the foundation of all knowledge: the immediacy of sense perception or observation. Basically it was already a matter of dispute in the beginnings of the Vienna circle whether the so-called basis statements of a scientific theory possess a distinctively certain character. At any rate, the notion of the protocol statement was soon shown to be insufficient for grounding such a distinction. Such distinctiveness can be achieved only in terms of the function of sentences within the totality of a given theory. That, however, is in the end a hermeneutical principle: that the particular thing is just as much determined by the whole as is the whole by the many particulars. Thus the logical form of induction could not withstand a more acute critique. It was the merit of the Vienna Circle's criticism of itself to have realized that the justification of knowledge, in the sense of a certitude removed from all doubt, was an impossible task. It is true that scientific theories possess their meaning and their validity in the end only by reason of the confirmation of which they are susceptible through experience. But cognitive certitude is achieved less in virtue of a cumulative series of confirmations than by the continuing absence of counterinstances that would amount to falsification. It was a coherent sharpening of the logic of confirmation when Karl Popper raised falsifiability instead of verifiability to the status of a logical condition of scientific propositions.[15] Actually the real process of research is not confined to this self-certification *e contrario*. But it seems to me that the fruitfulness of scientific questioning is defined in an adequate manner if it is really open to answers in the sense that experience can refuse the anticipated confirmation.

Consequently it does not seem to me at all contradictory to the logic of inquiry when Thomas Kuhn elaborated the significance of the paradigm for the progress of research.[16] His theory of revolution in science rightly criticizes the false linear stylization supposedly connected with the progress of science. It shows the discontinuity effected by the dominance of any given time of basic paradigmatic frameworks. The whole problem area of the relevance of questions depends on this, and that constitutes a hermeneutic dimension.

Similarly the path of constructing an unequivocal scientific language capable of reconstructing the logical structure of the world came up against difficulties. In the end, the vanquishing of the nominalist ideal of a complete correspondence between linguistic sign and referent brought about the downfall of the idea of ultimate grounding in this line of inquiry as well. Especially Wittgenstein's self-critique and his conception of the language game opened up a completely different mode of approach.[17] The univocal scientific language was replaced by the primordial relationship to practice of all speaking. In this way the logical task of grounding knowledge was transformed into the philosophy of the so-called linguistic analysts, who attended to the logical analysis of the most diverse modes of speech and language games. At least in principle, therefore, the primacy of theoretical speaking in statements was restricted. And this, too, is ultimately a hermeneutical principle: that the way any given utterance, discourse, or text is to be understood depends upon its particular scope. In other words, if it is to be understood correctly, one has to understand its scope.

Finally the theory of trial and error that Popper worked out is not at all confined to the logic of specialized inquiry. Despite all the foreshortening and stylizing in this schema, it makes plain a notion of logical rationality that reaches far beyond the field of scientific research and describes the basic structures of all rationality, even that of practical reason. At any rate, rationality is not only to be understood in terms of the rationality of means with respect to a pregiven purpose. It is precisely the pregivenness of our ends, the whole build-up of the common purposive directions of our social existence, that underpins the practical rationality that is confirmed in its critical appropriation of the norms of social conduct that determine us. In this manner, too, practical rationality has to make use of the manipulative possibilities with respect to the world of means placed at our disposal by science.

At any rate, one has to ask oneself here whether all these movements in the direction of dedogmatization, inasmuch as they have been understood by logical empiricism itself as theory of science or as the mere expansion of scientific modes of procedure, are not subordinated to an instrumental ideal of knowledge. By this I mean whether linguistic analysis or even the description of logical rationality is subjected to the ideal of the science whose analysis they describe. This means that it is erected as a means and an instrumental scaffolding for the progress of knowledge. This would, of course, be a limit to their self-understanding and to their justification and scientific inquiry itself would be the first to refuse to follow them. Taking seriously the task of philosophic justification with which they are occupied would require going beyond this boundary. It was a grand insight when Wittgenstein noticed that language is always in order. But it would imply a technological misunderstanding of itself if this insight were to be confined to the task of correctly distinguishing language games and of dissolving illusory problems. Language's being-in-order is far more. Wherever it is doing what it is supposed to do (which is to actuate its communicative function), it does not work like a technique or an organon for reaching agreement with oneself, but it is itself this process and content of coming to agreement, even to the point of the buildup of a common world in which we speak an understandable — no, the same — language with one another. This is the linguistic constitution of our human life, which can be neither replaced nor repressed by any information techniques.

Thus we see shown forth in the sciences themselves a hermeneutic dimension as a properly sustaining and grounding factor — in the natural sciences as the dimension of paradigms and of the relevance of one's frameworks of inquiry. In the social sciences a similar structure might be described as the self-transformation of the social engineer into a social partner. In the historical sciences, finally, it is at work as the ongoing mediation of what was once before, what is now, and what will be tomorrow.

In the historical sciences the apparent opposition of the knowing subject and his object is eliminated. It is not merely a restriction placed on that rendering anonymous of knowledge that we call objectivity; rather it is a distinction that it experiences insofar as the historical knowledge of the past sets us before the totality of our human possibilities and therewith mediates us along with our future. That is what we should have learned from Heidegger's violent thought experiment of thinking being as time and of opposing the "hermeneutics of facticity" to the idealism of a sheer understanding of a meaningful tradition: that the traditions within which we stand — and every tradition that we creatively or appropriatingly pass on — offer less an objective field for the scientific mastery of a subject matter or for the extension of our domination by knowledge of the unknown than a mediation of ourselves with our real possibilities engulfing us — with what can be and what is capable of happening to and becoming of us.

And so science is no less science where it is aware of the *humaniora* as its integrative function. Just as little is the scientific character attainable in the natural or the social sciences lost by reason of the fact that the theory of science allows them to be aware of their limits. When this happens, is it "theory of science" or is it "philosophy"?

Notes

1. Neo-Kantianism is a collective name for philosophic movements that brought about a renaissance in philosophy in the last third of the nineteenth century through a return to Kant. Its two most important directions consisted of the Marburg School (chief representatives are H. Cohen, P. Natorp, and E. Cassirer) and the Southwest German school (chief representatives are W. Windelband, H. Rickert, E. Lask, and B. Bauch). The former oriented philosophy toward the exploration of the cognitive conditions and principles of the natural sciences; the latter directed its attention chiefly to the problem of value and beyond this toward the philosophic grounding of the *Geisteswissenschaften* (*Kulturwissenschaften*). Both schools blossomed in the period before World War I.

2. The foundational work of Immanuel Kant (1724–1804), *Critique of Pure Reason* appeared in 1781 (a second, revised edition appeared in 1787); in 1783 there followed the *Prologomena to Any Future Metaphysics Able to Claim to Be a Science*; and in 1786 the transition to a genuine metaphysics of nature, *Metaphysical Elements in the Natural Sciences*. Kant's most important ethical works are *Foundations of a Metaphysics of Morals* (1785), *Critique of Practical Reason* (1788), and *The Metaphysics of Morals in Two Parts* (1797). The third of the chief critical works, *Critique of Judgment,* appeared in 1790.

3. John Stuart Mill (1806–1873) presented a theory of inductive method in his work, *A System of Logic, Rationative and Inductive* (1843). He started from the notion that all universal concepts are abstractions from sense experience. The German translation by J. Schiel (Braunschwig, 1849) exercised a widespread influence and introduced the term *Geisteswissenschaften* for the English "moral sciences."

4. Auguste Comte (1798–1857) divided the history of humanity into three stages: a theological, a metaphysical, and a positive, in the last of which the metaphysical is dissolved by science. (Chief work, *Course of Positive Philosophy,* 6 vols., 1830–1842). Both the logical apriority of the Marburg Neo-Kantians and the logical empiricism prepared in the writings of the Scottish philosopher David Hume (1711–1776) took up a stance critical of metaphysics.

5. Edmund Husserl (1859–1939); *Logical Investigations.* vol 1: *Prologomena to a Pure Logic* (1900); vol. 2: *Explorations towards a Phenomenology and Theory of Knowledge* (1901). "Transcendental" phenomenology was unfolded in *Ideas towards a Pure Phenomenology and a Phenomenological Philosophy* (1913), *Collected Works* (*Husserliana*) 16 volumes to date (The Hague, 1950ff.)

6. Rudolf Carnap (1891–1970) published in 1928 *The Logical Construction of the World* (2d ed., Hamburg, 1961). Carnap was one of the founders of the Vienna Circle, which emerged with the programmatic publication, *The Scientific World-view — The Vienna Circle*; the journal *Erkenntnis* promoted the program. Other representatives of Neopositivist philosophy were M. Schlick, L. Wittgenstein, O. Neurath, and H. Reichenbach. They connected up with the earlier Positivism, especially the "empiriocriticism" of R. Avenarius (1843–1896) and E. Mach (1838–1916).

7. René Descartes (1596–1650): *Regulae ad directionem ingenii* (*Rules for the Direction of the Mind*) (written in the 1620s, published in 1701); *Discourse on Method* (1637); *Meditationes de prima philosophia* (*Meditations on First Philosophy*) (1641); *Principia Philosophiae* (*The Principles of Philosophy*) (1644).

8. J. G. Fichte (1762–1814), F. W. J. Schelling (1775–1854), G. W. F. Hegel (1770–1831).

9. Hegel's chief works: *The Phenomenology of the Spirit* (1807); *Science of Logic* (1812–1816); *Philosophy of Right* (1821); *Encyclopedia of the Philosophic Sciences* (3d ed., 1830).

10. Plato: *Phaedo* 99c/d.

11. Hermann Lotze (1817–1881), physician and philosopher, was one of the most influential authors and teachers of philosophy in the nineteenth century (an early *Metaphysics,* 1841, and *Logic,* 1843, which appeared in newly elaborated form in *System of Philosophy,* 1874 and 1879, followed *Microcosm* 1856–, to mention only some of the most important works). Eduard Zeller (1814–1908) was known especially in virtue of his great work, *The Philosophy of the Greeks* (1844–   ); he made his entry into the academic world with his lecture, *On the Significance and Task of Epistemology* (1862), published with addenda in his *Lectures and Essays, Second Collection* (Leipzig 1877), 479–526. He fashioned the word *Erkenntnistheorie* as a new designation for the foundational philosophic discipline

(cf. A. Diemer, *art.* "Erkenntnistheorie, Erkenntnislehre, Erkenntniskritik I," in *Historisches Woerterbuch der Philosophie*, vol. 2, ed. J. Ritter (Basel, Stuttgart, 1972), col. 683.) Opposed to the university professors, there stand Arthur Schopenhauer — well known for his bitterness toward the guild of philosophers (1788–1860) (chief work: *The World as Will and Representation,* 1819); and Friedrich Nietzsche (1844–1890) whose ideas first achieved real influence in the twentieth century.

12. Wilhelm Dilthey (1833–1911): *Introduction to the Geisteswissenschaften* (1883); *Ideas Concerning a Descriptive and Analytic Psychology* (1894); *The Types of Worldview and their Construction in the Metaphysical Systems* (1911), besides numerous works on the history of ideas. On the historical school and Dilthey's philosophy, see H.-G. Gadamer, *Truth and Method* (New York: Seabury, 1975), 153–234.

13. E. Husserl, *The Crisis of the European Sciences and Transcendental Phenomenology* (1962): See. H.-G. Gadamer, "The Phenomenological Movement," in *Philosophical Hermeneutics,* trans. and ed. David E. Linge (Berkeley: University of California Press, 1977), 130–181, and "The Science of the Life-World," in *ibid.,* 182–197.

14. Martin Heidegger (1889–1978): *Being and Time* (1927, 10th ed., 1963).

15. Karl R. Popper (1902–): *Logic of Scientific Discovery* (1934, 3d German ed., 1969); compare E. Stroeker, "Aspekte gegenwärtiger Wissenschaftstheorie," in *Wissenschaft/Wissenschaften. Philosophie aktuell* ed. H. Holzey (Basel/Stuttgart 1974), vol. 3.

16. Thomas S. Kuhn, *The Structure of Scientific Revolutions* (1962).

17. In his *Philosophical Investigations* (1935), Ludwig Wittgenstein performed this self-critique upon the conceptions he set forth in *Tractatus Logico-philosophicus* (1921). Several volumes of Wittgenstein's writings are now available.

Index

Galileo, 6, 70, 155–156
Geisteswissenschaften
  as a dimension in science, 115
  epistemological grounding of, in
    hermeneutics, 39
  grounding of, in concept of value,
    40
  and heritage of metaphysics, 146–
    147
  hermeneutical foundation of, 130
  transcendental grounding of, 152
  and unity of dialogue and dialectic,
    47
German Idealism, 30
Goethe, Johann W. von, 21
  doctrine of color of, 23
  and organic unity, 22
Grass, Günther, 24
Greece
  affect of moral philosophy of, 123
  and concept of utopia, 80–81
  foundation of philosophy in, 5
  relationship of theory and practice
    to philosophy of, 89–90
  self-consciousness in philosophy of,
    15–16
  theoria in philosophy of, 17–18
Gris, Juan, 43

Hebel, Johann Peter, 93, 113
Hegel, Georg W. F.
  absolute knowledge and, 49
  acceptance of, in Europe, 43
  allegiance to Greek philosophic and
    scientific tradition of, 159
  ambivalence of Heidegger toward,
    55–56
  analysis of problem of time by, 62
  and application of dialectic to
    history, 36–37
  Aristotle's legacy in, 42
  characterization of philosophy by,
    16
  claim of reconciliation of faith and
    knowledge in, 28–29

  common consciousness in, 32–33
  and community of language, 3
  comparison of metaphysical
    philosophy of Greece and 35–36
  and concept of absolute knowledge,
    38
  and concept of honor, 32
  concept of reconciliation in, 34–35
  and concrete universality, 49
  conflict concerning Christian
    character of philosophy of, 29
  criticism of Kantian moral
    philosophy by, 31
  definition of philosophy of, 29
  doctrine of determinate negation
    of, 82–83
  doctrine of pastness of art, 28–29
  and experience of alienation
    (*Positivität*), 33–34
  Heidegger and, 42, 55, 61–62
  and idealism of freedom, 51
  indispensability of, for philosophic
    thought, 29
  influence on the arts of, 43
  influence on Heidegger and
    Cassirer of, 41–42
  interpretation of theology of, 27–29
  meaning of "reality" in, 36
  and metaphysics, 3, 51–52
  and natural science, 10–11
  partisan division in interpretation
    of, 2, 27–29
  philosophy of world history of, 9
  and reason in history, 39
  reason for rapid breakdown of
    philosophy of, 25
  resistance within philosophy to
    dialectic method of, 39–40
  self-consciousness and, 15, 31–32
  speculative displacement of the
    proposition in, 57
  study of system of needs by, 12–13
  theory of objective spirit of, 40
  universal synthesis of, 56
  view of labor of, 75
  view of philosophy and empirical
    sciences of, 7